CRAVING
for
TRAVEL.

CRAVING *for* TRAVEL

Celebrating Life's Moments

✦ JIM STRONG CTC, ACC

Craving for Travel

Celebrating Life's Moments

For information, please contact:
Brown Books Publishing Group
16200 North Dallas Parkway, Suite 170
Dallas, Texas 75248
www.brownbooks.com
972-381-0009

ISBN-13: 978-1-934812-48-8
ISBN-10: 1-934812-48-X

LCCN: 2009928702
1 2 3 4 5 6 7 8 9 10

Photography: A special thanks to all of those who contributed to this book.

"Traveler's Song" reprinted by permission of Ada Limón.

This book is dedicated to the twins,

James and Jennifer—present and future world travelers.

Contents

Happy Birthday to Me:
Impeccable Settings for Celebrating Your Life

Family Recipes:
Places Family and Friends Adore

No Pictures Please:
The Splurge before Your Wedding

Let's Do It Again:
Hideaways Offering New Memories

Traveler's Song
by Ada Limón

Take your good self with you,
Pack your ticket in your heart.

Begin at your familiar doorway,
For here's where the world starts.

Let the globe's spinning song
Come seduce you, soft and low.

Take your good self with you,
The thrumming earth says, Go!

Foreword

Travel is the finest way to celebrate life's significant moments, a gift that only improves with the passage of time. A safari where the sounds of the African bush echo in your sleep, a cruise back in time on the Nile or the Yangzi, a villa in the hills of Tuscany—all treasured memories to share with family and friends.

As you read this book, think of a coming milestone—a birthday, anniversary, retirement or other special occasion—that calls for the celebration of a lifetime. The pleasure of sharing a remarkable travel destination lingers through the years as you, your family, and friends remember the fun and the camaraderie of spending time together.

If romance is your inspiration, creating the scene for a proposal means finding the perfect blend of privacy and a spectacular setting. When romance progresses to a wedding, celebrate with an unforgettable journey for two. Then as you build a life together, birthdays and anniversaries offer the opportunity to explore the world—and indulge. When you reach the stage of life where you are looking back on treasured times, revisiting the sites where you and your family spent time together will build on those special memories, and bring new surprises.

Whether you are celebrating a honeymoon, anniversary, graduation, family reunion, milestone birthday—or simply spending time with loved ones—I hope the ideas in this book will inspire your own extraordinary journeys.

Geoffrey Kent
Founder, Chairman, and CEO
of the Abercrombie & Kent
Group of Companies

"You belong together, and you belong here."

A Guaranteed Yes

Faultless Settings for Your Proposal

Hôtel Plaza Athénée Paris

*C*reate an unforgettable, heart-melting moment when she first touches the engagement ring. When that special hour takes place in Paris, you trace the enchanted footprints of lovers who came before you, and those steps lead to the breathtaking Hôtel Plaza Athénée. At the crossroads of the Champs-Elysées and the graceful, tree-lined Avenue Montaigne, the occasion becomes an instant to cherish. Immortalize it.

This house of beauty stands between the Eiffel Tower and the Arc de Triomphe with all the elegance of the Venus de Milo in the Louvre. Outside, fashion, entertainment, and business merge, but inside, sophistication, luxury, and innovation fuse to ignite your passions into fireworks. Since you decided to come this far, go all the way.

The spectacular elegance of the hotel entices the world's elite, but the directeurs have not been content to offer staggering, incomparable views of the Eiffel Tower. A complete redecoration now flawlessly blends the unsurpassed opulence of the past with a magical "Plaza Red" theme that greets you at the front façade. The expert staff members anticipate your every need and escort you into eight floors that feature 146 guest rooms and forty-five suites. If you are drawn to the

delicate balance of refinement and lavishness, the spirit begins here.

Characterize luxury as the opportunity to have your choices displayed on a pallet. The hotel serves up several categories that delight everyone. The first six floors redefine Louis XVI and Regency décor, and the top two floors envelope you with new dimensions in Art Deco. Life feels wonderful within the Plaza Athénée.

A perfect setting for lovers, the Terrace Eiffel Suite boasts two entrances, a living room, dining room, a large bedroom, a marble bathroom, and a steam room. Picture windows overlook a staggering, 360-degree view of the Paris skyline from the privacy of a terraced roof or through an opaque glass wall of the bathroom that magically becomes transparent at the flick of a switch. The Art Deco style has been carefully crafted to reflect the Eiffel Tower. Rich and luxurious powder-blue silks and velvets enhance chocolate-colored mahogany furniture and floors. Discover heaven against a brilliant backdrop of blue Paris skies.

When Edith Piaf sang "La Vie en Rose," she could have been describing the Royal Suite, one of the largest in Paris and the quintessence of art de vivre. This distinguished and graceful dwelling overlooks the Eiffel Tower and the glamorous Avenue Montaigne. Dressed in silks and embroidered fabrics, this exceptional suite beckons you through two entrances, greets you through a reception hall, and welcomes you into a double living room. Become lost in luxury with eight televisions, four bedrooms, four marble bathrooms, two Turkish baths, private dressing rooms, and a Jacuzzi. You will not want an early morning wake-up call.

Celebrate chic exclusivity and savor award-winning cuisine within the Athénée's fantastic Alain Ducasse Restaurant. If you like to vary your tastes with your mood, three other dining venues and Le Bar du Plaza Athénée do more than provide access to atmosphere; they endow extravagances both day and night.

After a late night, revive your youthfulness in the Dior Spa. A combination of innovation, refinement, and stimulation of all five senses reveals the intimate possibilities of spectacular renewal. Emerge radiant, refreshed, and toned to perfection.

At the Hôtel Plaza Athénée, the tenderness of a private home and the warmth of the city of lights await your answer to the question, "Will you marry me?"

The Carlyle

New Yorkers claim to be a different breed of people. They walk fast, talk fast, and think fast. When you are inside the Carlyle, you feel as though you are a genuine New Yorker. You can be confident that your marriage proposal will be accepted quickly. Things happen that way in New York.

No tower rises more distinctively among the stunning panorama of skyscrapers than the Carlyle. It was built swiftly, and as one of the finest examples of Art Deco artistry, it has surpassed the test of time. Outside, just one view of the inspiring icon makes the impression of a lifetime. Inside, everyone from the concierge to the elevator operator knows your name. The ravishing black-and-white marble floors and butterscotch-gold upholstery in the lobby usher you into a dazzling citadel of comfort. This tasteful Manhattan landmark offers an elegant private atmosphere, the finest cabaret entertainment, and an enviable location brilliantly positioned on Madison Avenue in the East Side pied-à-terre.

Any fiancée melts like butter after checking into an Empire Suite, where spaciousness blurs the line between a hotel room and a residential apartment. The Royal Suite spreads out an elaborate expanse of hominess and caters to your whims

with a cozy cocoon for two. When you treat your love to a night at the Carlyle, your romance will be recognized.

In the Big Apple, a wealth of museums, galleries, and upscale shops await mere steps from the Carlyle. Central Park, naturally lovely in any season, spreads its beauty within easy walking distance just one block away. Fall in love with the treasure of possibilities.

The Carlyle's doors open to all the excitement the city has to offer, but you may not want to leave. The essential element of true satisfaction can be habit-forming, and their permanent residents know this.

At the Carlyle, you feel as if you are in an elegant, private home. The refined interior style owes its uniqueness to an inimitable roster of famous designers. Recent updates uphold the hotel's venerable design heritage while adding a distinctive touch of contemporary panache. Baby grand pianos, imported rugs, and rare linens abound, but they may not engage your attention for long. Stupendous views of Central Park from the secluded terraces make you forget you are among millions of people. English poet John Donne, who said "No man is an island," never stood inside the Carlyle.

A romantic dinner for two in the Carlyle Restaurant marries opulence with intimacy. Designed by Mark Hampton in the style of an English manor house, the seventy-seat restaurant intimately arranges plush chintz-covered banquettes, Aubusson rugs, and mirrored alcoves against a dramatic six-foot-tall floral arrangement. English hunting scenes by Fores, as well as engravings by Redoute and Liliacae complete the country house ambiance, but the menu will promptly seize your attention. Greek and classic French influences take hold of your taste even if you are not planning to think of food on the happiest night of your life.

Immerse into Sense, a Rosewood Spa, and forget the hurried beat of the metropolis. Let the world go away, while you cast adrift on a sea of tranquility. The enchanting Yves Durif salon forbids time to intrude on your personal adventure into body and mind renewal. Experience what most tourists will never know.

The city that never sleeps reaches a nightly crescendo in the cabaret setting of the intimate Café Carlyle. Sink into the pastel-printed upholstery and let your eyes wander over the whimsical wall-to-wall murals by renowned Moulin Rouge artist Marcel Vertes. Tap your fingers to the legendary Eddie Davis Jazz Band. After the last applause, tuck yourselves away in the seclusion of the Bemelmans Bar then greet the sunrise over Central Park as it cascades its colors into your memories. At the Carlyle, romance takes on many shades.

Set the tone for wonderful years to come when you propose at the Carlyle. Be assured that your offer will be rewarded with an immediate union. Things happen that way in New York.

The Isle of
Eriska Hotel

*Y*ou may hear wedding bells as you near this hidden island off the coast of Scotland. Beyond the land where the white saltire cross of the Scottish blue flag unfurls over the bonny lochs, there are nearly eight hundred islands, and only three hundred of them are inhabited. One of these islands rises from the North Sea to reveal a breathtaking, sweeping shore. On its horizon peek the turrets of an old castle designed by architect Hippolyte Blanc and built in 1884 by a branch of the Stewarts of Appin. The new owners welcome you to the Isle of Eriska Hotel, an escape from the rest of the world and a perfect setting to invite the love of your life to be yours forever.

Raise a Scottish whisky toast to your future in the opulent comfort of this private three-hundred-acre island. Indulge in the charming interplay of old-world magic and cutting-edge sophistication when you discover your plush, private cottage suite and its enchanting setting within secretive gardens. The Isle of Eriska Hotel provides an extraordinary location to make your proposal unforgettable.

Inside the baronial big house, the resplendent billiard room resonates with voices from the past, and the click of billiard balls can be heard beyond the door where a delightful maze of

twenty-five beautiful bedrooms in varying shapes and sizes play host to enthralled new guests. Each setting has the facilities and amenities you expect and the loving realization of intimate promises.

Can you imagine the two of you alone by candlelight in the conservatory built beneath the boughs of a centuries-old oak tree? Servers tend to your tranquility while you contemplate whether to pop the question before or after dinner.

In their Stables Restaurant, dining menus open to the best authentic Scottish meals ever prepared. Oysters, mussels, and home-smoked salmon are delivered by shellfish boats directly to the pier. By candlelight or sun-drenched morning, temptations tantalize you.

When your first day as an engaged couple dawns, enjoy the variety of activities that give the two of you time to rest and explore the island. Beyond the main house, retreat to the well-appointed swimming pool to relax and unwind. The Howard Swan designed golf course challenges you to beat the pros if you can ignore the spectacular views of the Western Isles. Because so many choices proliferate, just follow your whims.

Get away and become one with nature. A short stroll to the sea leads by an ancient bridge where a picturesque setting awaits commemoration on film. Wander along olden trails carefully marked with white signposts. Your new life together promises to take you down many paths.

Begin the journey of a lifetime and listen to the wedding bells chiming in your heart. Be confident your tender proposal will be joyously received at the Scottish Isle of Eriska Hotel.

The Ritz-Carlton, Moscow

Moscow has long been a meeting place for lovers, and the Ritz-Carlton fondly reinvents the tradition. History may echo throughout the Russian capital, but now a stylish shadow is cast on the Red Square, where class, fashion, and sophistication compete with old-world standards. The Ritz-Carlton doors frame the perfect setting to say "I do."

The dawn of a new era in comfort springs gallantly from this eleven-story tower of grandeur perfectly positioned on the famous Tverskaya Street, Moscow's main avenue. Experience the enchantment of this luxurious palace overlooking the city's abundant architectural, historical, and cultural wonders. The Ritz-Carlton designers have unveiled a contemporary décor of polished, dark cherry and burl wood, bathrooms finished with marble from Portugal and the Altai Mountains, and a Presidential Suite with large floor-to-ceiling windows overlooking the Red Square. Beauty has never been so bold.

For the most magnificent choice to suit your stay, the Ritz-Carlton Suite adoringly opens to an elaborate setting for lovers. Floor-to-ceiling windows face the Kremlin, Red Square, and St. Basil's Cathedral. Classic furnishings exude

Russian imperial style. Dazzle yourselves with the entertainment possibilities found in the spacious living room with a grand piano, dining area, and library. In the Ritz-Carlton Suite, every guest feels like royalty.

Memorable dining opportunities exceed guests' expectations in Jeroboam. Discerning palates discover inspiration in the cuisine vitale prepared by international chefs. Every appetite finds fulfillment with flair, and the artful dishes make a proposal in Moscow an evening to remember.

As your spirits soar, ascend to the rooftop, where a secluded, urban oasis on the stylish terrace of the 02 Lounge affords an altogether more casual and upbeat adventure. Enjoy the city without leaving luxury behind. The heart-stirring views of the Red Square at night and trendy music from around the globe under-score the sensation that you have found a secret domain.

The Ritz-Carlton experience enlivens the senses, instills well-being, and fulfills even your unexpressed wishes and needs. Their promise bespeaks a credo accomplished with pride and zest. In this overwhelming ambiance, you may find it hard to get a clear perspective on local culture and life. If a definitive perception eludes you, beauty and diversity will not. You can be sure your proposal will be accepted when you offer it inside the Ritz-Carlton Moscow. You belong together, and you belong here.

Cap Estel

For a match made in heaven, never compromise on where you propose. At the end of the nineteenth century, Prince Stroganov of Russia became captivated by the splendorous view of the Mediterranean from a private peninsula perched on a promontory between Nice and Monaco. For the pleasure of his true love, he built an original palace far below the cliffs and along the ocean. Recent enhancements have majestically transformed the villa. Every great love story should begin at Cap Estel.

Cap Estel is the epitome of luxury and elegance on the Côte d'Azur. Enter through wrought-iron gates, and from there, descend to a grand palazzo, where divine designs, spacious rooms and suites, and breathtaking ocean vistas inspire the two of you.

Cap Estel bestows many settings to celebrate your engagement. Take pleasure in stimulating hours on the sunny private beach or by the seawater infinity pool. Stroll hand in hand through lush Riviera gardens without another soul in sight. Dream of joys to come, while you live a lifestyle reserved for royalty and celebrities. At Cap Estel, your destination becomes your destiny.

Treat yourselves to an impeccable escape. Let the days you have been dreaming of begin with all the excitement of driving a new Ferrari along the Riviera coast. Chic contemporary bathrooms, white Egyptian cotton bed linens, and the fluffiest of toweling bathrobes are exclusively yours. In top-floor suites, bask on incredibly large sun-drenched terraces, but as the shadows lengthen, let chilled champagne mellow the tone of the evening.

If you think like a celebrity chef, the guest-only restaurant tenders an ambiance that answers your unspoken demand. In the special hour before you propose, savor the singularly unique dish the chef creates just for you, the flawless service delivered with an air of discretion, the immaculate locale, and the Mediterranean menu with delicious surprises. Cap Estel makes a potential groom's or budding bride's heart soar.

Expect to look back on your stay at Cap Estel as the place where the infinite possibilities of never-ending love blossomed in blissful seclusion. On your big day, your promise will be confirmed because you have discovered the right place at the right time. You have never felt this way before.

Château Les Crayères

Y ou resolved to make a perfect world yours forever. Entice your one-and-only to Château Les Crayères, a storybook address nestled discretely in the heart of Reims, the city where the world's greatest lovers pledge their vows. The age-old, French château with just twenty rooms and suites blends tradition with comfort and refinement. Inside its doors, a feeling of intimate sophistication envelops you, and simplicity and elegance perfume the atmosphere. At the Château Les Crayères in France's Champagne region, fragrant love blooms as gorgeously as flowers in spring.

Take notice how your passion changes when you first set sight on the enormous gardens surrounding the estate. Tall and gracious maple, fir, and chestnut trees dip their boughs to the two of you on the eve of your engagement. Encircling gardens welcome you with their gracious spread and suggest the chic style that awaits you inside. While proposing a life together, discover the best at the Château Les Crayères.

Imagine making your glamorous entrance in the grand foyer with its regal staircase. Give in to the temptation to kiss beneath the grandiose and poetic Chagall that overlooks the setting. Pierre-Yves Rochon enriched the décor with cozy

lounges and a beautiful English-style bar rich with deep shades of green. All around you, others occupy quiet corners, and they seem to know the secret the two of you share. Savor the moment and remember it forever.

Two French words perfectly describe the regal and dramatic personal accommodations: élégance and plénitude. A haven of stylistic refinements and douceur de vivre, each room lovingly sets a style of its own. Feel blessed when ensconced in one of the lovely Princess Suites' calming bathtubs as you gracefully recline beneath inspiring garden-facing windows overlooking the Reims cathedral. Vivid décor and private garden-side terraces instill tranquility in the rooms of this traditional French hôtellerie. Be enchanted.

If you plan to propose while you are near friends and family, the divine moment glitters when dining in the belle époque restaurant. The rare combination of charm and cuisine in this luxurious gourmet retreat plays against a milieu of carved walnut paneling and tables overflowing onto a terrace. Whisper your big question beneath a gigantic white parasol while breezes murmur from the gardens and woods and softly echo the telling moment. Complete the night with a toast to the future. Your world may change, but Château Les Crayères remains as constant as the stars.

Love should take you places where you've never been before. When you recall Château Les Crayères, looking back will never be lovelier.

The Chanler at Cliff Walk

Cliff Walk, along the eastern shore of Newport, Rhode Island, combines the rugged natural beauty of the shoreline with the architectural history of the town's gilded age. Wildflowers, birds, and scenic vistas all add to this delightful walk, but where the picturesque trail leads to the Chanler, the path to romance begins.

Majestic iron gates welcome you into splendidly landscaped gardens where irresistible feelings of devotion subdue your sense of history. Unmatched affection characterizes the grace and grandeur of this getaway where guests feel soothed, spoiled, and sequestered from the world. The atmosphere endows plentiful opportunities for the unveiling of your engagement ring. You bring the jeweled promise of commitment; the Chanler affords the inspiration.

Romantic dreams spring to life when you sweep beneath a portico and into the timeless, sparkling lobby. It bespeaks splendor, welcome, and comfort. Built about 1873, Cliff Lawn Mansion was the first house constructed on Cliff Walk, but the echoes of history have given way to awe-inspiring, newfound opulence.

Celebrate time spent in your resplendent chamber. Stunning antiques and authentic furniture from a bygone era grace the period themes of each of the twenty rooms. An abundance of breathtaking fabrics mesh together to provide delightfully compelling eye candy. Lovers repose with a butler-drawn bath, a moment in time with rose petals, bath salts, candles, and Spiced Pear Champagne. Emerge into the warmth of your fireplace and exquisitely hand-painted tile murals.

No one visits the Chanler only to sleep, but these rooms inspire heavenly dreams with their intimacy, charm, and affluence. Most rooms feature skylights and canopy beds tucked beneath original oil paintings or antique prints. Your cozy hideaway opens onto a private patio overlooking the ocean, the perfect backdrop for the moment when you agree to unite your lives into one. Savor the seclusion.

The Chanler attributes a large portion of its renown to the Spiced Pear Restaurant. Tuscan dishes, fine wines, and a scintillating atmosphere form the perfect compliments to the accolades you cherish when friends learn of your engagement. Consider your table for the setting to spring the big question. Those around you will delight as you share the love.

When you emerge from the charms of the manor into the ambiance of the world, breathtaking sightseeing, shopping, and sailing adventures accompany the dawn of your new life together. Collect memories you will never forget. The timeless allure of the Chanler enhances your vision of your future together.

"The paradise enriches your soul and energizes your spirit."

Walking the Aisle

Romantic Venues for Your Wedding

The Inn at Palmetto Bluff

Your perfect day requires a perfect setting. The Inn at Palmetto Bluff hosts a wedding as only an Auberge Resort can—with world-class service, gourmet catering, professional event planning, and award-winning accommodations in South Carolina.

Your guests arrive at the quaint Village Square, where the glow from antique gas lamps announces evening. To the right stands the stately River House, where final preparations are stirring for the celebration to come. The promise of a remarkable experience fills the air.

Your wish for the most breathtakingly romantic setting imaginable comes true in the Waterside Chapel. Its simple design highlights the spectacular natural beauty of the location on the banks of the May River, where a stunning view through the stately arched windows reveals the gathering waiting eagerly. You are about to become the bride of your dreams.

Your exchange of vows heralds the launch of a memorable reception, and here, a selection of delightful venues are spread before your fingertips. The Wine Cellar holds more than four thousand vintage wines. Original artwork, dramatic lighting, and a stone fireplace set the stage for an intimate reception

everyone will recount. Let your guests amble. More surprises are footsteps away.

At the height of the party, your friends will discover that the River House dining room offers an inspired culinary experience with exceptional South Carolina Low Country cuisine infused with exotic local flavors and updated with a contemporary flair.

If the crowd flows outdoors, entertaining and dining at Moreland Landing comes with an unexpected delight: an incredible five-story tree house wrapped around a centuries-old live oak tree. At its roots, a traditional oyster-roasting pit overflows with the delicate aromas of an old-fashioned Low Country feast. Your chef can give vent to his culinary surprises. The inn outlays an impressive stone fireplace by sculptor Wayne Edwards for a one-of-a-kind finishing touch on your perfect day.

After rice cascades over the bride and groom, unwind and rejuvenate your entourage. They can nestle into fifty cozy cottages and cottage suites designed in classic Colonial style, reflecting the region's architectural heritage. Pine floors, vaulted ceilings, and verandas with spectacular views lull them into the serenity of a private hideaway. Their talk may be about you, but their thoughts are enraptured with their stay.

For families attending your wedding, one of the two-, three-, or four-bedroom Village Homes ensures accommodations worthy of revisiting. Spacious rooms with vaulted ceilings and hardwood floors are luxuriously appointed. Each home has a full kitchen generously equipped with appliances, fine glassware, and silverware.

The Inn at Palmetto Bluff proposes an escape created by nature and perfected by Auberge Resorts. The paradise enriches your soul and energizes your spirit. Your wedding may commence as an event to remember, but it concludes as the ideal beginning of a new life.

Château de Mirambeau

As a waltz enlivens music, Château de Mirambeau enriches weddings. Illuminate your celebration by inviting your guests to a dream world floating between the vineyards of Cognac and Bordeaux. Create a mood of colorful opulence in this magnificent setting amidst lovely villages and architectural treasures. Lift the lively atmosphere to an innovative intensity. At the Château de Mirambeau, the art of design reaches a new plateau.

Pomp and circumstance have long been part of life at the Château de Mirambeau. Kings, princes, and ambassadors appreciated the château before the Count of Duchatel donated the building to the world. Grace your wedding with the importance of a state event when you sweep down the aisle. Italian chandeliers, enormous gilt mirrors, flounced curtains, and ornate candelabras add touches that set the stage for a ceremony your guests will cherish. The original towers, galleries, spires, and stone porticoes transport them back in time to savor the ambiance of ancient days. The suites are adorned with elegant Renaissance motifs and are inlaid with refined antique furnishings, canopy beds, and marble bathrooms. Happy endings begin at the Château de Mirambeau.

Activities abound for recreation and pleasure. Come with your companions to chat in the cozy lounge. Invite your inquisitive friends on intimate walks beneath aged trees in the park. Call the courageous ones to soar above the vineyards in a hot air balloon. Guide the golf enthusiasts to any of the twelve courses near Bordeaux. Tempt the tennis devotees to a challenging match. Beckon the bikers to daring excursions. Magnificence of this scale cannot be revealed instantly. Discover the majesty over time.

Your festivities become as sumptuous as the bouquet of a full-bodied Bordeaux when the hotel stages an exclusive wine tasting event in the restaurant just for you and your guests. If you have a secret obsession for arranging a night everyone will talk about for years, the Cognathèque's renowned cognacs, as well as its celebrated cuisine, can be served outside on a terrace beneath the stars.

Let your love blossom in a medieval castle where the utterly charming interiors shimmer with a light and color that spills out across the magnificent courtyard, sharpening your fascinating plunge into a past rich with art and history, making your wedding wholly unforgettable. Exchange vows at the Château de Mirambeau. The empire belongs to you.

Hacienda
de San Antonio

*I*f life were a wedding cake, the Hacienda de San Antonio would be the icing. The coral pink hotel in Mexico's small highland area of Colima serenely displays its new decorations as if it were trying to outshine the jaw-dropping landscape of coffee plants, blankets of bamboo, and the awe-inspiring backdrop of the Colima volcano. Love may be the finest flower in life's garden, but the manicured grounds and formal gardens filled with fig and cypress trees are a dreamy, award-worthy oasis.

Love's young dream can be found inside the elegant arched buildings. The name strikes romance—Hacienda de San Antonio. The authentically restored nineteenth-century plantation estate emits exclusivity and passion. One of Mexico's best-kept secrets, the mountainside retreat elegantly occupies five hundred acres in the pleasant highlands beneath the shadow of the Volcano de Fuego. On the day of your wedding, may your joy soar higher than its peaks.

Evoke endless love when you take your vows in the hacienda's ninety-year-old chapel. Walk radiantly down the aisle and through the inner courtyard beneath a canopy of apple, orange, and lemon trees in the sculptured Spanish gardens. For a wedding written in pure Latin poetry, Hacienda

de San Antonio keeps some of its old traditions alive. The best and most beautiful things in the world cannot be seen or even touched. They must be felt with the heart.

Every couple desires precious time alone. Wild parrots sing for you when you are carried over the threshold of El Sol, the largest of the hotel's suites. Once wrapped in the hacienda's luxury, savor the soft puffs of hardwood-scented smoke floating gently up to the vaulted brick ceiling. Throw open the French doors to your balcony. Toss the bridal bouquet to the eager señoritas gathering in front of the African tulip trees lush with tangerine-colored blossoms. Sit side by side in the moonlight and gaze upon your future together. All you have to do is dream.

Celebrate the occasion with wine and sweet words. The staff of more than seventy-five never misses an opportunity to refill a wine glass at your reception. Surround the two of you with friends and family in the dining room in front of the castle-sized fireplace. Let the party spill out onto the rooftop terrace, under canvas umbrellas bordering the view of miles of rolling hills stretching down toward the lush volcanoes. Guests may enjoy both international and Mexican cuisine prepared with organic fruits, vegetables, and locally produced products. The only stress will be saying no to all the pampering.

When newlyweds smile, everyone knows why. Your exquisite wedding has transported you out of the real world. Join your hands and your hearts at the Hacienda de San Antonio.

Calistoga Ranch

*T*ake the wedding world by surprise. A grand, natural setting in the Napa Valley sets the stage for a marriage ceremony with intimate, under-stated elegance. Calistoga Ranch, a remarkable Auberge resort, secludes expansive country living within 157 acres of remarkably pristine land. Say "I do" to the harmony of singing birds and wedding bells tucked away in this hamlet.

Anticipate the pleasure of introducing the love of your life to the lodges. A scenic drive from San Francisco Bay transports you to an idyllic, vineyard-speckled canyon where the perfect union of ancient oaks, majestic hills, and a historic town fits as snugly as a wedding band.

Attract everyone to a wedding uniquely fashioned to your own tastes. Your guests are escorted past a lovely pergola to the main building, which houses the casual but chic reception area. On nights when the valley cools, an outdoor lounge with a crackling fireplace lends a fun and lively touch to the gathering. The informal yet modish mood recalls the moment you first realized your love for one another.

Highlight the affair with impeccable service, fine cuisine, and first-rate amenities. Calistoga Ranch offers an authentic

Wine Country experience that guests will warmly recall for years. A professional staff attends to every detail, including menu selections, technology needs, rooms, and activities. Surround your vows with an ambiance that colors the moment you express your love to one another with the perfect shades of romance.

Staging the wedding of your life goes beyond a perfect gown. Hosting a gathering at Calistoga Ranch lets your friends and family celebrate and feel at home. Hidden in a hillside, the Wine Cave opens up a marvelous setting for a dinner and reception. A vaulted ceiling and vintage chandeliers overhang enough space for dozens of people to enjoy a foretaste of what beauty the two of you bring into the world.

After a shower of rice, Calistoga Ranch puts everyone to bed in lodges graced with a soothing, California aesthetic. Situated along the banks of Lake Lommel with a mountain forest backdrop, warm redwood, oak, and pine accents bring the outdoors into expansive living areas. Slate floors, handwoven rugs, and custom-designed furniture offer private getaways for every family and individual.

Close friends and family find that being in the place of your dreams thrills as much as seeing you in love. The one-of-a-kind Estate Lodge offers the ultimate indoor-outdoor experience. A private, two-bedroom home nestled near the Lakehouse anticipates what your lives will be like together. As you step into the 2,400 square feet of indoor living room and outdoor living room and bath, make yourself at home with a roaring fire, full kitchen, and dining area. Enjoy relaxing moments in your hot tub at this great start to your journey together.

Bring everyone together for a festive dinner. The Lakehouse dining room, overseen by a notable chef, overlooks a panoramic, private lake. Alfresco dining and exceptional vintages exquisitely express the depths of your love. Gracious dining beneath open-beamed ceilings and a canopy of amber lights creates a romantic dinner or a lavish party.

Promises come true at Calistoga Ranch. Let its rich luxury and sophistication enhance the foundation of your union.

Kamalame Cay

*O*nce you have found the perfect mate, toast to your bright future with a wedding where heaven and earth meet in perfect harmony. Nestled above a rocky bluff and looking out on the pristine turquoise waters of the Bahamas, Kamalame Cove embraces the sounds of the wind in the palms and the softly massaging surf. Surrender to them.

Introduce your family to the great love of your life at a private beach hotel crowning a peninsula attached to Andros Island by three miles of sugar-soft sandy beach. The island escape draws you into a mind-set that calls for only bare feet, suntan lotion, and a champagne cocktail, making Kamalame Cay the perfect hideaway to exchange vows amid romantic splendor.

Your beach cottage decked out with flowers becomes a wonderful nest where you can wake up to the aromas of buttery croissants and warm coffee in the morning. Even the smallest waders on your guest list can find a swim spot in the private cove. Let them collect sand dollars and shells while you prepare to walk down the aisle.

Begin your new life together over a quiet dinner in Kamalame Cay's intimate dining room, a picnic on a nearby cay, or a

table for two right on the beach where servers attend to your every need. Welcome your guests to diving, tennis, and Caribbean touring adventures. Spend lazy mornings at the freshwater pool or take romantic walks beneath dazzling sunsets. The possibilities are as many as the sandpipers hugging the palm trees.

When you are at Kamalame Cay, the sun-kissed isle shores reach to your doorstep. If your guests value casualness and isolation, charm them with bedrooms and baths that spread through an entirely separate wing. Complete villa suites and intimate cottages built from native stone and filled with Indonesian furniture offer inviting verandas,

wood beam ceilings, and oversized soaking tubs with ocean views.

Kamalame Cay's over-the-water spa concentrates on restoring and rejuvenating body, mind, and soul. An experienced spa team personalizes distinctive treatments to ensure that you receive complete relaxation. Every visit becomes a journey into serenity.

For the bride dreaming of a beachside wedding surrounded by pristine scenery, buffeted by gentle breezes, and serenaded by softly lapping Caribbean waters, Kamalame Cay unveils an idyllic setting where nature and nurturing combine for a wedding of unforgettable beauty.

"When exquisite interiors compete
with the masterpiece of nature, only you can
select the outcome."

1 + 1 = 3

The Consummate Locations for Romance

The Tides
Riviera Maya

When the heat of passion meets the warmth of romance, the ignition becomes electric. Souls merge effortlessly in the seductive Tides Riviera Maya resort. The blissful paradise extends along seven miles of pearl-white sand nestled just outside Playa del Carmen, Mexico. Secluded deep within sultry woods, the opulent hideaway harmonizes with the primitive Maya jungle. Something untamed and wild filters through the tropical foliage. Permit the sensation to overwhelm you.

The light of love sparkles in the intimate and serene splendor of thirty private villas, a stunning spa, and an award-winning restaurant and lounge. Lovers share more than nature, ancient cities, and archaeological ruins. When distant stars twinkle through gently swaying palms, night breezes hint at limitless possibilities. Listen to them.

Guests are personally welcomed and led through the forest along a path to where the stucco, palapa-roofed bohíos snuggle beneath starkly beautiful foliage. Your discovery begins where private plunge pools are surrounded by luscious jungle gardens and hand-crocheted hammocks swing languorously in the breeze. Then, the aesthetics transform from primitive to plush. One step through the louvered mahogany doors and

you notice that the pristine qualities of the dramatic jungle give way to spacious, air-conditioned interior comfort. Sisal rugs and canopy beds with hand-stitched Egyptian cotton linens, duvet covers, and glorious down pillows are outlaid for passion. Separate bathrooms with airy showers are poised to cool and cleanse. An entertainment center conceals a dreamy collection of romantic music to color the moonlit night with song. The ocean's poetry whispers in the background, and the sea keeps secrets.

At dawn, the mystic, natural beauty of primeval woodlands awakens with the aroma of freshly baked breads and banana leaves simmering beneath the earth. They herald the poetic dining experiences being prepared by chefs in La Marea. The scent of Mediterranean, Mexican, and Mayan cuisine rich with the traditional flavors of achiote, chiles, pumpkin, fresh lime, and chaya tint the air with a tempting fragrance. Special dishes for your private dining are generously prepared on an outdoor, ancient Mayan kitchen made of wooden branches, and the chefs are delighted to teach you the nuances of native cooking.

Dine anytime, anywhere. It may be hard to choose between a beachside lunch after snorkeling coral reefs or a poolside dinner in the solitude of the exclusive Presidential Villa, but the morning to near-midnight room service will come to you. Uncork any of the more than eight hundred bottles of vintage wines from the wine cellar. Remember you have no appointments the next day.

Romance becomes magical in the tender ambiance of the Fertility Ritual House. Experience the ancient Ritual de Fertilidad performed to the sound of drums in a rustic wood cabin adorned with colorful Maya decorations. This ritual stimulates the senses with a treatment made of chia seed, high in folic acid and essential to both your body and the development of a healthy baby. Honey produced from the anise-scented xtabentún flower tenders nectar said to intoxicate you from neck to toe. A shaman accompanies the slow, relaxing massage with ritual blessings performed using traditional Mayan copal incense. Drums, maracas, and Mayan music enfold you in the soothing purification rite. Surprise your senses.

In a place of enchantment and unfettered elegance, where the sand, sea, and jungle cast untold spells, the seduction of the Tides Riviera Maya opens a portal to passion and speaks to your soul.

Capri Palace

You first realize that someone loves you when eyes reveal the thought. At the Capri Palace, the emotion radiates from you. The feeling flows as you adore the bold designs, vivid colors, and landscaped gardens. The sentiment surges when you see the elegance of the columns, arches, and vaulted ceilings of its classic Mediterranean architecture. You reflect their passion when you first gaze from the palace to the Bay of Naples and the endless sea. On a clear day, you can see Vesuvius endlessly smoking. The flame of romance glows within the Capri Palace.

Residing over the ruins of a great Roman palace built by Emperor Augustus, Capri Palace stands as a stronghold of soul, and it has withstood the test of time. Couples discover the palm trees and pool overlooking the Isle of Ischia are a glorious outdoor living room when the charms of their suite can no longer contain their spirits. The allure of canopied beds, marbled and tiled bathrooms, and softly textured ecru-colored furnishings entice lovers to explore the secrets of their souls, but the call of the world beckons as the lighthouse on Punta Carena summons seafarers. When exquisite interiors compete with the masterpieces of nature, only you can make the choice.

Light plays with shadow when it lingers within the Megaron Suite, a huge penthouse with a private circular swimming pool set in a Mediterranean roof garden. Two of the hotel's deluxe rooms, as well as five of their suites, also have private pools and gardens. If you choose the top-floor Acropolis Suite, the sea view divulges why past emperors chose the isle for wooing their secret loves. The stunning view overlooking the Mediterranean invites you to daydream, if fantasy dominates your imagination. If you find inspiration in the eyes of the one who adores you, let Italian indulgence encourage his ideas. People in love and the Capri Palace are peerless.

Rendezvous for intimate moments in the awarded L'Olivo Restaurant, where discerning gourmet chefs create Mediterranean specialties that set the tone for an experience to cherish. Comfortable armchairs, private fireplaces, and library areas offer friendly gathering nooks, and when paired with vintage local wines from the cellar that holds more bottles than Italy has vineyards, any occasion becomes an affair to remember.

The Capri Palace harmonizes with the land and proves that magical moments do not happen by chance; they take place because someone loves.

qualia

*A*ustralia comes of age with qualia, a sea of love for those seeking the most romantic and warm hideaway in the world. Located on the secluded northern tip of Hamilton Island, indulgence as a lifestyle assumes uncommon dimensions in this place of outstanding natural beauty. The ocean envelopes the resort as if it were the arms of your true love. Give yourself over to absolute pleasure.

Fragrant eucalyptus pervades the pavilions that are nestled in perfect harmony with the splendor of the Great Barrier Reef. The resort immerses you in a relaxed atmosphere where everything has been meticulously considered to enliven the senses and encourage romance. They call this mood "the qualia effect." Let it lure you.

When time stands still, love takes root. A truly special place, the area possesses a relaxed and mesmerizing calmness that almost makes clocks irrelevant. The landscape distinctively embraces the accommodations and virtually infuses each local timber and stone selected for the designs. This freedom to become one with the terrain enables you to enjoy rooms four times the size of ordinary hotel rooms. At qualia, love flourishes.

Harmonize with architecture and each other. The Beach House, their ultimate in seclusion and privacy, bestows spacious entertaining areas for those times when romance takes a backseat to gathering with friends. Furnished interiors and fabrics with patterns inspired by nature enrich the setting with an ambiance that accelerates attention to enjoyment. A separate guesthouse invites close contact with others in your party, and the island serenity always draws you near to enjoy the great loves of your life. The blessing of private sundecks exposes the warmth of the sun and captures amazing sunset views. Wide eaves and breezeways shaded by eucalyptus trees create the opportunity for both.

Add two restaurants to the expansive, postcard views of the wide sea and Whitsundays, and the medly emerges as a fresh and innovative experience. Dining at Pebble Beach may be at the

water's edge, but the chef's passion for fresh and seasonal Australian produce rides on the cutting edge of greatness. Combine that with unique spa treatments, such as "Bularri Yarrul," a massage using ancient hot stones and selected Australian handmade essential oils, and the two of you experience luxurious relaxation like never before.

Light the sparks for lively afternoons on the sun-drenched island. Expect the ecstasy of sandy beaches, scuba diving, snorkeling, and sailing. Feel time unravel however you choose. Return to the elegance of qualia when the inspiration overcomes you. The lifestyle may become habit-forming.

Charm your sweetheart with an irresistible invitation to qualia and the Great Barrier Reef. From the sound of water breaking on the Coral Sea shore to the soft breeze that sighs across the point, qualia calls you to rediscover romance.

Four Seasons Resort Langkawi

*L*ove will always be mysterious. Fully awaken your capacity to love when the two of you arrive at the Four Seasons Resort on Langkawi Island, Malaysia, one of ninety-nine islands in the Andaman Sea. A seventh heaven of lush rainforests, rocky limestone cliffs, and beachside Moroccan tents inspires the excitement of mutual discovery. If your soul craves seclusion with the one you adore, your journey comes to romantic fulfillment here.

The Four Seasons Resort sprang up on the site of an ancient coconut plantation, and here, the excitement of Malaysia explodes with a fascinating fusion of cultures. The architecture resembles a traditional Malay village, with a grand entrance that comes straight from an ancient Thai temple and a domed reception room that reminds you of an Arabian sultan's palace.

The whisper of ocean waves grows quiet when you cross the threshold of your lavish personal villa sequestered within lushly overgrown garden foliage. An oversized living area reflects modern Malay designs, and a breathtaking veranda opens to the sun-kissed surf. Your villa's concealed plunge pool and reflecting pond seclude the two of you in clandestine showers that evoke the feeling of a tender, tropical rainfall. Surrender to ecstasy in the spa with six private, self-contained treatment pavilions. Beyond your domain, tennis courts, an infinity pool, and a gym offer an alluring array of temptations to take hold of you.

An unforgettable, exotic dining experience awaits you on the beach. Under starlit skies, enjoy a private, romantic evening with your loved one in a royal tent from Rajasthan, India, embellished with traditional lanterns, handwoven Indian durries, oversized divans, and fragrant tropical flowers. These surroundings make passion impossible to subdue.

In Serai, the celebrated restaurant that means lemongrass in Malay, the creative menu features light, classic Italian specialties, using the freshest ingredients, delicately balanced with aromatic herbs and spices drenched with Mediterranean flavors. The emerald waters of the Andaman Sea are never lovelier than when set in the background of an open-air dinner. Let the sea breeze snuff out the candles.

Love arises in the heart, and when the situation calls for a tryst near pristine reefs off the shore of a modern town with a majestic past, the Four Seasons Langkawi nurtures the occasion.

Palms Place Hotel & Spa

Palms Place Hotel & Spa, Las Vegas, the newest addition to the Palms Casino Resort, showcases living in Las Vegas as you thought it should be, welcoming you with eye-popping levels of splendor transcending that of any luxury experience in America. Without ever setting foot on anything but Brazilian ebony and marble, you walk from one panoramic view of the Strip to the next. It may take a roll of the dice to choose which room, suite, or penthouse excites you the most.

No wonder the stars are attracted to the Palms Place. The penthouses achieve perfection on an ostentatious scale, carefully balancing grandeur and indulgent intimacy in a manner that makes every minute utterly unforgettable. If you can picture yourselves luxuriating in your own private cantilevered clear glass pool dangling high over the glittering city, you are ready to tease your senses with an experience that transcends all other sensual escapades in America. Only you know the degree to which you are prepared to be spoiled.

In the best of modern living, you feel less like a guest and more like a resident. The SkyTube, an elevated, enclosed moving walkway, provides guests of Palms Place with direct access to the Palms Casino Resort. Be careful, you may not want to leave.

Tickle your nose with champagne bubbles while peering out at the city from a height of fifty stories in the Ghost Bar. When the music moves you, find an open space on the dance floor at Rain, the hottest dance club in Las Vegas. Watch a sexy poolside lounge transform into an outdoor nightclub at Skin, and then escape to the truly decadent spa for rubdowns that do for your body what you wish your one-and-only could do.

The resort's dining options are equally extraordinary. Alizé, the snazzy rooftop lounge, offers gourmet meals and floor-to-ceiling views of the sparkling Strip at night. Little Buddha brings out exquisite cuisine served beneath crimson, gold, and celadon decorations outlaid beneath the watchful gaze of a giant Buddha statue. The resort offers some of the best nightlife in town with a constellation of casino choices to astound anyone, but romance does not take a backseat to revelry.

Be sure and leave an open page in your diary. At the Palms Place, Las Vegas, a storybook romance waits to be written.

Château du Sureau

osemite may be renowned for its waterfalls, grand meadows, and ancient, giant sequoias, but a mere eight miles away, the Château du Sureau shines as a brilliantly cut diamond on hay-colored foothills and thickets of stately pines. Here the classic traditions of old Europe etch exquisite traces in the chateau.

Beyond wrought-iron gates, nine acres of meticulously landscaped meadows embrace the stately château. The stone turret adorning its walls, the stately arches entwined with topiaries, and the tall cypress trees waving their boughs all seem to beckon you to a place where love vanquishes time. Delightful interiors hold true to European hospitality. Expect no front desk or check-in. The owner and her warm human touch guide you through the Grand Salon where a limestone spiral staircase invites you to discover your lover's chamber. A floor-to-ceiling fireplace and a circular music alcove create an affectionate mood to match your own feelings. Sense the subtle yet unmistakable touch of love and pride.

Get ready to fall in love again. In the Château du Sureau, ten intimate rooms are named after fragrant herbs and flowers grown on the estate,

and each offers a delight to the senses. Yours proffers European elegance with impeccably styled European antiques, sumptuous fabrics, fresh-cut flowers, and oversized soaking tubs. Your faces glow with firelight and gentle conversation. Let new dreams take wing. Tomorrow can wait.

There lives in each of us a secret quest, an undying passion for the exquisite. A short stroll from the Château along a softly lit garden pathway leads to Erna's famous Elderberry House restaurant. A quartet of dining areas is illuminated by arcaded windows and antique chandeliers. The menu tunes melodiously with the gentle cadence of the seasons. Enjoy the essence of romance.

Should you venture beyond Château du Sureau, explore each other beneath Yosemite's awe-inspiring waterfalls. Feel their power energizing the air. The falls create misty gales and an atmosphere of freshness and vitality as grand as the nearby grove of giant sequoias.

Deep in the core of your characters, the two of you share adoration. Deep in the soul of the Yosemite Valley, the Château du Sureau stands as a shrine to tranquility. Time spent here seems more precious than anything material.

The Nam Hai

You journey to Nam Hai to be fashioned by what you love. Together, the two of you are encircled by a seemingly unbroken swathe of alluring, soft white sand. A thousand distant lanterns glowing reds, blues, greens, and yellows are buffeted by gentle breezes on the China Seas. Softly lapping water serenades you along the beach. You are one with each other and the universe.

Your desire to become closer has brought you to a tranquil stretch of the timeless ocean fringed with coconut palms. Nam Hai's landscaped gardens welcome you to a lush oasis away from busy Saigon and Hanoi. The splendid resort sprawls across a playground near historic Hoi An, and an unobstructed vista of the Cham Islands affirms that you are not in an ordinary beachfront getaway. Nam Hai opens its doors to an intimate world dedicated to the ultimate in indulgent luxury. Welcome to a haven of serenity.

When love and skill work together, expect a masterpiece. Etched in tradition, the fine work of ancient artisans takes on renewed life at Nam Hai. The essence of spaciousness and understated charm covers the Vietnamese architecture. The touch of clever planning and attention to detail reflects in the finishes, fabrics, and frills. Nam Hai cunningly combines

traditional shapes with contemporary ideas to harmonize with nature, just as the two of you complement each other.

Live and love the way you want. The power of life forces plays a part in creating an intriguing destination for lovers to linger in a transcendental experience. Discreet Vietnamese villas rest snugly around a series of horseshoe-shaped coves as if they are seashells in the sand. The single and multi-bedroom pool villas come with large bedrooms and eggshell-lacquered sunken baths that open to private outdoor showers kissed by the sultry air.

True love happens only once in a lifetime. Experience the pleasures of a private villa exquisitely set among tropical tranquility. The Nam Hai villas engage every sensation. Feel the delicate warmth of sea breezes and sun in your personal pool. See the languid islands on the remote horizon. Realize every inspiration with a mere call to your butler. Attentive service fulfills each wish.

Enjoy an intimate meal in Nam Hai's two gourmet restaurants overlooking the water gardens. Dark hardwoods, crystal, glass, and intricate brass work surround the two of you as you discover the delicate closeness you desire most. Become a poet and whisper something tender.

Only with the heart can one see rightly; essentials are invisible to the eye. Luxuriate in a fragrant petal bath in the tropical spa on a lagoon. Savor a cup of herbal tea, and then give yourself to a traditional Vietnamese massage. Asian holistic therapeutic treatments encourage you to revive your senses and satisfy your soul with nurturing in the total privacy of tantalizing Tibetan bathing rituals. Keep the fires burning.

Being deeply loved gives you strength; loving someone deeply gives you courage. Discover new avenues when you venture into Hoi An's bustling treasure trove of shops and landmarks. Hoan Kiem Lake, the Temple of Literature, and the One-Pillar Pagoda are just steps away from your Nam Hai door.

You feel love as you sense the whisper of breezes billowing over the China Sea. Saying "I love you" at Nam Hai comes easily.

The Wakaya Club & Spa

In a changing world, you instinctively desire to entice your great love to a place unaltered by the shifting sands of time. Wakaya Island in Fiji conceals a private hideaway tucked among 333 islands protected by coral reefs and isolated from the hurried world. The tranquility of island life embraces you from the moment you arrive, and you may wonder at first how to divest your cares and immerse in such unparalleled leisure. Love will find a way.

The Wakaya Club & Spa lays out a luxury private island resort unlike any other in the world. Gracious living, sophisticated cuisine, and freedom from hurry shift your focus to the most important part of life: becoming one with the person you have chosen to share your future. Here, you need no formal occasion to indulge in romance. Your two lives will be blessed by the harmony of an azure sea and your waterfront Fijian bure.

Each private bure indulges you in every conceivable comfort. The charms of a secluded rear garden and covered outdoor deck enfold the two of you in a world apart. A four-poster king-size bed clad in the finest sheets from Italy welcomes you into a private cocoon. Indulge in the spell cast by waves lapping against the shore and tropical songbirds cooing to the breeze.

Awaken to an open-air lava-rock shower in your villa high on a promontory overlooking the ocean. Trees laden with sun-sweetened fruit entice you to rejoin life in this remote and pristine corner of the world. When the island chefs prepare dining after dawn, waking up becomes a perfect pleasure, and feasting after sunset reminds you why food fuels the soul. Bountiful island catches and a bottle of wine make for a memorable presentation. The chefs understand the simplicity that underlies sophisticated cuisine; they know you have other thoughts on your mind.

On Wakaya, you can enjoy secluded beaches for swimming and picnics, plus a comprehensive selection of leisure activities. Be completely relaxed and spontaneous in planning your day. Court times, tee times, and dive times are wide open, and serenity, stargazing, and siestas are ever present. Renew your sacred promises in this tropical beach paradise, where the pounding rhythm of the sublime surf calls to each of your hearts. Couples come to Wakaya to explore life together. Here, nothing matters but the possibility of romance.

"Bring your love here and discover how near a new future can be."

Remember Me

Havens for Reconnecting

Hotel Splendido

Suspended high above the sea and framed by a ravishing landscape, an appuntamento at Splendido has been a favorite background for many years for lovers to rediscover their closeness. The ancient villa echoes with emotion, passion, and intrigue. Elevate your relationship to heightened dimensions on this picturesque hilltop overlooking the Italian Riviera.

Originally a monastery, the four-story building follows the contour of the hill so that all principal windows face both sun and sea. Standing amid verdant woodlands overlooking a ravishing seascape, the Hotel Splendido blends beauty and comfort with a kaleidoscope of nature's earthy colors. A living postcard, every corner reawakens the senses, conveys emotions, forges memories, and forms a bond between places and people. After your initial embrace, ascend to splendidly appointed rooms and suites that compete with the magic of the Mediterranean to enfold you in a timeless spell.

A sophisticated blend of elegant décor, relaxation, and exclusive comfort becomes obvious once you enter the Presidential Suite. Pastel colors, tromp d'oeil artwork, and olive wood parquet floors sway you with visual appeal. Three magnificent terraces overlooking Portofino's cove and the Gulf of Tigullio entice you to harmonize with the ambiance. Splendido promises to inspire the two of you to entirely new devotion.

For private moments, walking paths lead you through olive groves, gardens, and vineyards. They show the way to steep slopes that dive cleanly into the deep Ligurian Sea. They guide the two of you into shady forests with pines overhead, chestnuts underfoot, and ferns all around. They direct you along trails to a hidden monastery in a tranquil cove. Follow these ancient paths and rekindle forgotten passions.

At dusk, begin a night of reunion with a cocktail served on the panoramic Bar Terrace. Once the moon glows brightly over the sea, take pleasure in a traditional peasant seafood dinner in the Ginepro Room. Unleash the flavors of Italian cuisine with homemade pasta and aromatic herbs influenced by the chef's imagination. Be aware that dinner on a terrace overlooking Portofino can beguile you. Remember the reason for your stay.

Utopian climate, hidden gardens, and Riviera excursions will entice the two of you to reconnect Splendido-style.

Dar Ahlam

Share a sense of quest with your partner. The thrill of a journey to uncover the secrets of a nineteenth-century Moroccan Kasbah fills both of you with the desire to travel. Dar Ahlam, perched between the town of Skoura and the Atlas Mountains in what was a sultan's private hunting ground, rests at the gateway to desert adventure. Mark a date in the dunes on your calendars. Invite your partner to join you in an oasis of olive and palm trees.

The drive from Marrakesh to Dar Ahlam will transport the two of you to the most luxurious property in Morocco. As you wind your way around twisting mountain roads through a terra-cotta-toned landscape, buildings that look like oversized sandcastles suggest that Dar Ahlam unveils pure theatre and a flirtation for all the senses.

Superb service, unforgettable food, and splendid accommodations flourish among the beauty and exquisite simplicity of the Berber countryside. The fortress conceals a labyrinth of luscious gardens with a T-shaped stone pool and outdoor massage tents, all designed by French landscape architect Louis Benech to look like a magazine cover composition. In 2002, the palace was revitalized, and now a house of dreams stands where every detail ensures that your

ability to forge new memories with your partner comes true.

This adobe palace strives to surprise. Its striking architecture impresses you with the majesty and the softness of the colors reflected by the surrounding space. Light gives the citadel an aura of a museum. The dominant characteristics are space and quietude. Splendid suites and villas enriched by brick grounds and cob walls frame the vast openness with pure and audacious décor. Prepare to receive the gift of a lifetime as you commemorate your relationship.

Moroccan heat waves disappear when you are swathed in the beauty of old-world charm. Sit in the elegant lounge with its billowing gold-edged muslin curtains and sexy fireplace. Authentic wonders come to life when you admire gardens from a hammock or wander the silk-curtained corridors. Clever lighting designs change according to day or night, revealing different aspects of the building. Intriguing features resonate from every corner.

You will find nothing ordinary about the Dar Ahlam suites. Each villa encircles a central patio and includes a large drawing room, dining room, and traditional lounge. Your terrace with outdoor fireplace overlooks your private plunge pool. Televisions are unnecessary. When you experience the excitement of watching Atlas Mountain peaks reaching to clouds that shower rain on the fertile Sahara valley, nature orchestrates entertainment more vivid than any screen can contain.

Dine like a sultan. The extensive Dar Ahlam menu combines traditional specialties with the latest in culinary innovations. Chefs serve inspired meals on your terrace, in your garden, or by the pool. Take a champagne picnic to the Valley of Roses with the hotel's excellent guide, or stage a candlelight dinner out in the desert to stargaze while you stir cocktails. The show-stopping sunset, breathtaking in the golden twilight, looks different each night you dine in another location.

Ultimately, you remember the dreamlike quality of Dar Ahlam. There are so many new beginnings worth celebrating. The two of you will agree: Dar Ahlam overwhelms with moods that weave romantic notions. Imagine the thousand and one temptations.

Four Seasons Tented Camp Golden Triangle

*D*raw near to one another again when you escape from the real world to the sweet land where Thailand, Laos, and Myanmar (Burma) form an incredible "golden triangle." A remarkable journey unravels before you to bring you through the secluded Thai jungle to the pristine, unspoiled Four Seasons Tented Camp Golden Triangle, a lavish realm elevated high above the banks of the Ruak River. A bronze map beneath your feet marks the route a long-tail ferry boat will take to transport you from the exotic Four Seasons' thatched-roof reception dock to the remote, landscaped grounds of the camp. A gong waiting at the camp entrance gives a welcome full of Eastern promise. Here in the heart of the untouched jungle, the air is rich with the luscious fragrance of a sea of tropical flowers, and butterflies and birds circle contentedly overhead. The steady, low crushing sound of elephants moving through the jungle creates a steady rhythm of life all around you. What a beautiful place to arrive!

Temper your beating hearts as you enter the Four Seasons Camp. The tents rise out of the jungle like a fleet of twin-mast schooners, a Bill Bensley design inspired by northern Thailand's hill-tribe villages. The fifteen freestanding tented

accommodations, with their perfect blend of rustic charm and plush comfort, are unmistakably branded with Four Seasons chic.

Right down to the hammered copper bathtubs, local artisans have decorated each tent with metal craftwork and antiques reminiscent of early jungle explorers. On handcrafted furnishings, primitive tools and old-world compasses point the way back toward love. The tents are comfortably distant from each other to allow for total privacy, and the open space of the large outdoor decks invites the two of you to share your adulation. An experience of such pure delight keeps the emotion fresh.

After testing your poise on a midday elephant trek, return to the camp via a suspension bridge to the remote spa hidden in the jungle on elevated stilts. Open-air *salas* feature rejuvenating traditional Thai massages and innovative rituals assisted by the healing power of mountain botanicals and warming spices, all to the soothing sounds of live singing birds.

Happy hour in the city does not compare to high spirits in the tropical woods. Each evening, guests trek to the ritual of cocktails, canapés, and cheeses at the Burma Bar by the light of a hundred torches. Divine cuisine inspired by Thai, Laotian, Burmese, and Western influences flavors the conversation as you indulge in your private seclusion. The Four Seasons Tented Camp Golden Triangle invites you to a one-of-a-kind opportunity to rekindle romance. Love rebounds beautifully the second time around.

Le Couvent des Minimes Hôtel and Spa

*Y*ou and your true love share a spiritual connection and you are alike in so many ways. Bring a new dimension to your relationship at a seventeeth-century hotel with a subtle combination of history, space, and comfort. Le Couvent des Minimes Hôtel and Spa gives you the added allures of high plains and hills, fields of lavender, and fascinating street markets where you can wander for hours. Rekindle your sacred bond at Le Couvent des Minimes in Provence.

No matter how many years have passed, your love of romance, history, and stunning countryside remains constant. Nestled on a hill in a stunning countryside drenched in sunshine, the graceful Couvent des Minimes has been beautifully redesigned out of what once was a monastery. Completely updated Flemish architecture with magnificently contemporary features sits superbly within terraced gardens. The original building dates back to 1613, but today, the modernized interior brilliantly fuses medieval architecture with present-day design. A new page of history has opened. Together, enjoy an enclave of happiness.

Memories may fade, but new experiences touch your heart and linger. A few centuries hardly separate you from

feeling the same kind of inspiration as the nuns when they stood within the vaulted cloister. Guest rooms are comfortably equipped to give a feeling of heavenly luxury. Great attention to detail and a gentle Mediterranean touch enliven all suites at the Couvent. Spacious terraces draw you outside to discover the serenity of the land. Uplift your spirits with an unforgettable view of lakes, cliffs, and the cultivated plains of the famous Gorges du Verdon canyons. Your true love will thank you for reuniting here.

When the temptation arises to leave Le Couvent des Minimes and explore the surrounding areas, enjoy easy access to nearby chic designer boutiques, ancient rustic villages, and quaint churches dating back centuries. Picnic lunches, biking, hiking, and horseback riding are all within reach.

At the end of the day, nothing surpasses the soothing comforts inside Le Couvent des Minimes. Talk things over in the quiet friendliness of the piano bar. Draw close with a game of pétanque on the hotel's own court. Relax at the charming indoor and outdoor swimming pools. During summer, the gorgeous courtyard and sunny countryside views entice you to forget time entirely.

Lose your cares in the Spa by L'Occitane, the first to open in France. Give yourselves over to pure indulgence in an exclusive beauty line of naturally sourced L'Occitane products that have been created for your pleasure. Talented spa therapists offer their heavenly sensations to restore your wellness and contentment.

Dining becomes a lavish experience at the two gourmet restaurants in Le Couvent des Minimes. Tasting local wines in the cavernous setting of Le Cloître can take hours before you indulge in the tradition of Mediterranean cooking that combines the delicacy of homegrown, natural ingredients from the enchanting Provence. A simple invitation to have lunch becomes a reaffirmation of why you became true lovers.

Riad El Fenn

Whether five or fifty years have passed, make good on your promise to love and cherish. Mysterious Morocco and the culture of Marrakesh weave an exotic fabric. An imperial city in the center of fabulous mountains that seem untouched by Western influences promises to place the two of you back on solid ground. Embark on a new beginning at the Riad El Fenn.

You can connect again when you enter together through the unassuming blue doorway of the Riad El Fenn and pass through three tropical courtyards outlaid with Carrera marble. Bestow a nod to the live tortoises and iguanas striking poses, as you drop a coin for good fortune into the fountain.

Slip up a tiny flight of steps that lead into the labyrinth of the eighteen-room fortress. The whimsically updated palace instantly surprises you with leather floors, floating staircases, and prints and paintings by famous modern artists. Marvel at the striking contrasts between traditional Moroccan architecture and refreshingly hip, boldly colored walls inspired by the rainbow hues surrounding the nearby Atlas Mountains. Riad El Fenn renews the spirit of love.

Enjoy exploring the gorgeous, sprawling oasis together. Have cocktails on the fantastic rooftop terrace decorated with woven-leather chairs, daybeds, and giant cushions. While you gaze at amazing views of the city and the magical, snow-covered mountain peaks at night, remember how much you enjoy each other.

You are different now, but you both still adore spacious, comfortable living. Your sorbet-colored guest suite with a king-size bed draped in Egyptian cotton linens, surrounded by scented candles, and accompanied by a huge array of babouche slippers reminds you of home. Sink softly into a sculpted tadlakt bath and rejoice that you took this journey to become close again.

For the ultimate in pleasure, revel in Suite 19. A glass-bottomed plunge pool on this duplex's private terrace forms the ceiling of the salon below. A cool mix of oriental furniture, antique mirrors, and Art Deco chairs makes for a memorable stay.

Begin each day with a blissful breakfast served anywhere you like. Plan a lunch in the cozy, informal dining room. Feast on lobster mousse and organic

produce gathered from an organic garden in the Atlas foothills. Chefs mix meats and fish from the city's daily markets to lay out a superb dinner highlighted with Moroccan and French wines. On the terrace by candlelight, the joys you remember about old times return.

Venture out in a horse-drawn carriage to Jemaa el Fna, the bustling central square. At sunset, the Koutoubia Minaret silhouettes against a vivid, crimson sky. Crowds throb with an overwhelming mix of musicians, fortune-tellers, snake charmers, and bustling market stalls. Nothing restores the beat of your hearts like the pulse of vibrant life.

After a few hours, the tranquility of the Riad el Fenn always draws you back. Unwind in the hammam, or spice yourself up with beauty treatments in the spa. A dual massage works wonders for restoring the excitement.

After you experience the mystical magic of Marrakesh, secure your close bond again and return to the real world contentedly. Riad El Fenn always lingers lovingly in your memories.

The Lodge at Blanket Bay

*R*evive close bonds by reuniting at the one spot on earth closest to Eden. The Lodge at Blanket Bay inspires awe the moment you look up and gaze on the grandeur of the glacier-capped Humboldt mountain range looming over the paradise with godlike splendor. Imagine the bliss you encounter when you first embrace at the Alpine lodges. Love rebounds beautifully when you are snuggled beside the bush-clad fringes of Lake Wakatipu.

You know you are at the bottom of the earth, but you feel as if you are on top of the world. New Zealand's finest corner distances itself just far enough from Queenstown and the ski crowds to seem like a world apart, but it takes only minutes to journey from the Central Otago wine region. You may land by helicopter, step inside onto heated floors, and be welcomed into the Grand Room with a drink by a huge fireplace of local schist stone that rises dramatically to the vaulted ceilings with exposed beams. Give each other a loving pinch. The spectacular views through enormous windows make you think you are dreaming.

Something familiar about the architecture dawns on you once you gaze on the handsome, heavy furnishing, vaulted wood ceilings, and aged hardwood floors. Blanket Bay

was built by an Idaho architect as a conscious homage to the lodges of the American West. Native New Zealand timber and stone and natural materials are showcased throughout, echoing the Lodge's bond with the environment. At Blanket Bay, the delicate blend of antlers and armchairs balances beautifully.

If you can keep from looking out the windows at the crystal clear lake and majestic mountains, luxuriate in a chalet stateroom's sumptuous furnishings. Lodge suites also reflect New Zealand colonial architecture and complement the main lodge with the use of schist stone and old steamer wharf timbers that seem to replicate the space that holds forth outdoors. A huge stone fireplace nearly dwarfs the king-size beds, and wraparound views from cozy chairs, balconies, and terraces entice you to sink into genuine peace and solitude.

Leave the lodge and begin a journey into the realm of glacier-fed rivers, green pastures, and sprawling grounds framed by the timeless towers of snowcapped mountains. Guests have plenty of enjoyable options to choose from during their stay. Bordered on two sides by national parks, Blanket Bay rests against a backdrop of rugged high country and ancient beech forests entwined with hiking trails. Experience a bird's-eye view of the breathtaking landscape with a scenic helicopter flight. Explore Arrowtown, a historic gold-mining village. Life takes on new dimensions when you add these adventures to your memories.

Thrilling culinary experiences unfold every night in the intimate dining room at whatever hour you choose. The Wine Cave presents private dining for cozy gatherings, and the Terrace unfolds award-winning cuisine within a magnificent setting with the roaring fire behind you.

Share a world filled with wonder, enchantment, and adventure. Resplendent rest and awesome scenery spread out such splendor that you may never want to close your eyes. At Blanket Bay, no stone is left unturned in the quest to provide the perfect luxury escape.

Canyon Ranch, Tucson

Long-term relationships and a lust for life seem to go hand in hand. Invite the love of your life to the magical Canyon Ranch, Tucson, where coyotes and roadrunners dash through cactus forests, rolling hills, and awe-inspiring mountains. Private time tailored to your interests invigorates the healthy feelings both of you crave. Give yourself the ultimate healthy living experience with experts who take control and help you celebrate the ecstasy of sensuality, sexuality, and passion.

The residential Casa Grande, the largest and most versatile accommodation, encompasses so much legroom, you feel as if the outdoors has been corralled under one roof. Twenty-seven hundred square feet of Southwestern style spread out enough space to include several bedrooms, an airy living space, and a full kitchen and dining area. Relax on your porch and take in the joys of a dazzling Arizona sunset. Dawn will awaken you to an exciting adventure in reunions, mutual discoveries, and a new you.

Your spirits will soar when you escape to adventure in the colorful Sonora Desert. Award-winning Canyon Ranch digs a foothold into the foothills near Tucson, where the contagious Arizona environment resembles a borderland postcard, inviting you to come explore. Sparkling streams and pine-topped mountains inspire you to tap into the full potential of your union and uncover that sense of camaraderie that you ache to rediscover. Unleash a healthy future in the sunny weather and matchless scenery.

If your passion for a sport motivates you to play better than ever, take your game to a higher level. Both novices and seasoned athletes grow with guidance from a team of expert coaches. Sharpen the skills, abilities, and mind-set necessary to improve all aspects of your performance. Perk up your golf game by training and conditioning with PGA pros on nearby courses. Change your game for good. Your friends will be amazed at your surprising transformation.

At the end of strenuous days, six gyms, a steam room and sauna, sunbathing decks, and whirlpools soothe, soak, and massage away tension. You both may agree to follow this regimen for the rest of your life. You come to Canyon Ranch to grow closer. Expect to emerge ready to take on the entire world.

"Celebrate the life in your years, not the years in your life."

Happy Birthday to Me

Impeccable Settings for Celebrating Your Life

Cuixmala

*T*he more you celebrate life, the more life gives you to celebrate. Gather your friends and family around you in the warmth of Cuixmala, where hot Mexican sand, water sports, and charming villas surround the event.

Enjoy an exclusive slice of the playground. Atop a high ridge overlooking vast, virgin acreage and the Pacific Coast, the road running south from Puerto Vallarta guides your friends through tropical forests where they hear the timeless roar of swells pounding the secluded beachfront. The naturally striking grandeur spreads over twenty-five thousand acres. Here, everyone creates new memories.

Enjoy a modern fairy tale in an enclosed wonderworld of its own. The hilltop view from the legendary Casa La Loma overlooks three kilometers of ocean beaches. More like a fantasy palace than any conventional villa, La Loma combines Mexican, Mediterranean, and Moorish architecture in an extravagant outlay of space and light. A palatial indoor dining room opens to a covered terrace with a pool-sized Jacuzzi that offers views of both the sea and mountains.

Ceilings soar to over twenty feet, with panoramic ocean views from both the bedroom and bathroom with its cozy

shower for two. A grand staircase leads to the saltwater pool, where lounging on the beach with unmatched personal attention accommodates your guests with the service of a private home. Permit the butler to serve your lunches.

Expansive hilltop villas, each with a cook and full staff, could comfortably accommodate a prince. Compliment your friends with rooms and ocean views that have played host to world travelers. The beautiful private villas blend light, proportions, and colors with space and panoramas of the beach, lagoons, river, and ocean.

In this peaceful environment, the beauty and freedom of nature meet comfort and service of the highest standard. Casa Alborada, a magnificent Moorish-style house, overlooks the coconut plantation and the Cuixmala River. A lavish, exotic garden surrounds Casa Puma with serene architecture that evokes a sense of peace and well-being. With your friends and family among the coconut palms, experience all that your heart holds dear.

Your birthday observes the reasons you are loved. Throw your biggest party with a celebration overflowing with organic foods cultivated on the property's ranch, orchards, and gardens. Explore the fascinating region on horseback rides among small herds of zebra and eland imported from South Africa. Swim in a private cove among palm trees at a private beach a few miles down the road. You spent a year earning these moments; relish the rewards at Cuixmala.

Vamizi Island Lodge

*I*f your birthday ranks as a milestone, start your new year off with a celebration hidden from the outside world but exposed to the blue Indian Ocean, powder-white sands, spotless reefs, and secret coves. The leisurely pace of Vamizi Island Lodge entices people who want to unwind and enjoy island life. Announce that you are inviting those you love to one of the last pristine and perfect places in the world. Give your family and friends a golden opportunity to express their love for you.

You instantly fall under the spell of Vamizi Island, located off the remote northern coast of Mozambique. Get swept away by the sound of an orchestra of birds filling the morning air with song. When you set foot in the sand and approach your beautiful beach villas, turtles race to the sparkling sea and monkeys peek at you from high in the treetops. The extraordinary site rivals your own uniqueness.

Sheltered shores play host to ten separate and secluded beach houses that Robinson Crusoe would have envied. Twelve villas face Rongui Island and hide discreetly behind concealing trees. Each boasts a large, high-ceilinged living room, a spectacular bathroom, and a veranda facing postcard sunsets and embracing cool sea breezes. Two are family-size

houses with double suites that can accommodate four people. In the large bedrooms, sink into king-size four-poster beds lovingly swathed in Egyptian cotton sheets and slumber until dawn heralds the coming of your important day. Instead of windows, look out through wooden lattice shutters that give rousing views of the ocean at sunrise. At Vamizi Island, quality defines your birthday.

Showing someone you care commences with a grand party in the thatched-roof main lodge. The décor mingles traditional carvings reflecting the area's Arabic influences, and they have the aesthetic detail of a Zanzibar palace. A sunset bar close to the water's edge animates the occasion for your family and friends. Personalize the special event by creating a memorable party themed around your passion for giving pleasure. Your imagination inspires genuine well-wishes.

The ocean holds the key to Vamizi Island cuisine. An emphasis on fresh lobster, prawns, calamari, and crab reveals the secrets of the Indian Ocean. Fresh local ingredients arouse your sense of flavor and tantalize your taste buds with Mediterranean accents. The wine list unfolds the best selections imported from a French vineyard belonging to one of Vamizi's owners. Pop the corks and give a birthday toast that glows forever in your friends' minds.

Spend entire days strolling along deserted beaches that slope gently into the sea. The island rates world-class dive site status. An incredible reef of unbleached coral close to the shore provides idyllic conditions for both snorkeling and scuba diving. Outdoorsmen in your group will cherish being among the first to engage in tag-and-release sport fishing in the reefs.

For those of you contented to experience barefoot luxury at its basic best, bike trails, cruises, and private picnics top the list of memorable possibilities. At Vamizi Island Lodge, your bright future shimmers as brilliantly as the glittering turquoise sea.

Borgo Finocchieto

A birthday at Borgo Finocchieto excites the way uncorking a vintage bottle of Italian wine stimulates: relaxation, diversion, and enjoyment abound. The welcoming enclave plays host for multitudes of events, and your birthday takes on a novel allure when staged within such a lusciously restored and tranquil setting. At Borgo Finocchieto, time stands as still as the ancient foundation stones.

For eight hundred years, the rocky walls of Borgo Finocchieto have anchored steadfast and strong between the Eternal City and Florence. Nestled on a rural hillside in the province of Siena on the historically significant Via Francigena, the Borgo has long been a stopover for adventurers. During a recent restyling, much of the old-world beauty was left untouched. Twenty-two new suites and magnificent gathering spaces now invite you to experience Tuscany at its best. They take your smile seriously.

Borgo Finocchieto combines the beauty and history of Tuscany in a tranquil setting where your birthday gathering celebrates all that makes you exceptional. Within this intimate and exclusive setting, let your family take over the entire village. Round tables on sunny piazzas call your friends to

gather, relax, and take in the beauty while filling their glasses with the best of local vintages. This portion of the province was immortalized in paintings by da Vinci and Lorenzetti. Create your own memorable portrait.

The Borgo has a total of twenty-two bedrooms within four freestanding houses spread out around a central piazza that functions as its own community. Gathering spaces include a formal dining room and outdoor dining terrace, a living room with grand piano and study, a media room, library, bar, conference facility, and ballroom for up to fifty guests. Partygoers adore revelry in the cantina and wine tasting room, and the interior arcaded courtyard hosts your celebrants with striking style. Individual suites are ample, luxurious, and private, while the public spaces encourage your friends to draw together. Expect a night to remember, but plan for days of festivities. Never rush the experience of a lifetime.

Your birthday celebration must feature a fabulous dinner. The cuisine and service at

Borgo Finocchieto uphold the Tuscan tradition of outstanding wine, delicious food, and friendly hospitality, but when other chefs are closing their kitchens, the feasts at Borgo are just beginning. They capture the essence of dining by preparing eye-popping wine and cheese smorgasbords and dinners inspired by you and your particular needs. Ingredients from Borgo's own gardens are harvested while the morning mist lays low across the valley farms. The reflection of dew still glistens on the grass as they enliven breakfast feasts outlaid to your specific desires.

Sumptuous dinners are typically three courses paired with selected wines. Spend a morning traveling with the chef to select produce in town. He embellishes the banquet with succulent sautéed shrimp, ravioli, and homemade pasta that rivals any festive Sunday family get-together. The memory of a classic dinner on the terrace becomes the best souvenir you bring home.

Borgo Finocchieto combines a tranquil setting with the beauty and history of Tuscany, an ideal pedestal for merriment in the cradle of the Renaissance.

Casa Nova

*C*ool conditions create warm hearts. No matter how old or young you become, rejoice over the happiness, love, and peace life has brought you. Gather friends and family around as you blow out candles at Casa Nova, a lovely, snow-kissed estate tucked snugly into the spectacular Deer Valley, Utah, mountain ranges.

The ski-in, ski-out mansion can play host to more than a dozen party guests with thirteen thousand square feet of space for living, loving, and laughing. Seven oversize rooms spread throughout four master suites, and ten fireplaces welcome you when the time arrives to come in from the cold. The Bunkhouse stacks eight bunk beds for cozy companions, and the attic bedroom even has a secret passageway that leads to three more beds. At Casa Nova, your friends provide hugs, and your host supplies surprises.

Casa Nova brings you the gift of awe-inspiring views of the Jordanelle Reservoir. Delight in the party you can have with a pool table, oxygen bar, and two hot tubs. Put a smile on all your guests' faces when they cross the threshold of a screening room stocked with an entertaining library of five hundred DVDs. A wood-burning pizza oven serves round-the-clock snacks, and a full spa offers the opportunity to gather and relax.

Get ready to party. Decorate the dramatic, domed ceiling in the Grand Room with balloons. Start the baby grand player piano to entice your friends away from the massive stone fireplace and the heated terrace and draw them onto the dance floor. Display your big cake on the ten-foot round table. Casa Nova provides all the decorations, food, and favors.

After the party, casual slope-side living can seem like a fairy tale at Casa Nova. Show your friends and family what a difference you make in their lives when you take them out on bobsled, snowmobile, and sleigh ride adventures at ski resorts just a short drive away. A private ski instructor meets you at your backdoor, and an on-call driver spirits you to all the local sites.

At Casa Nova, your birthday takes off with the flair of an Olympic downhill racer. Perfectly groomed slopes, cloud-like powder, and gold-plated service mix with imaginative indulgences to turn the event into an impressive experience. Celebrate the life in your years, not the years in your life.

Otahuna Lodge

Sophisticated world travelers would have bestowed a nod of appreciation for the largest private historic residence in New Zealand. For a birthday gala fit for a queen, make your procession to the winding road at the head of a secluded valley on New Zealand's South Island. Otahuna Lodge rests on a hill between the rocky outcrops of the Banks Peninsula. A long, meandering drive lined by stately oak, eucalyptus, and acacia trees leads to the lavish surroundings. The elegant country estate redefines prestige.

Otahuna Lodge was built in 1895 for Sir Heaton Rhodes, a high-profile Canterbury pioneer, and he resided in the three-story homestead for more than sixty years. Historians report that the Victorian gentleman was known for his enthusiasm for life. Crown your new milestone with a gala in the landmark lodge where the best just keeps getting better.

You enter a smart blend of classic atmosphere and lovingly arranged furnishings. Assemble your guests in the entry hall washed with a rich backdrop of mahogany paneling where a dramatic portrait of Rewi Maniapoto, a legendary Maori war hero, dominates the room. A roaring fire crackles near a stately, hand-carved, Kauri staircase. Lead your guests through vivid colors. Hunter green strié wall coverings garnish the entrance.

Pale blue wisteria garlands adorn the ladies' room. Punchy reds embellish the library. Marvel at the colorfully enhanced timber work throughout the house. Visitors notice the importance of a blush of tints in traditional interiors. You may have to remind them that they came for your occasion and not for the ecstasy of indulgence. At Otahuna Lodge, the surrounding splendor stirs up genuine bliss.

Some homes promise perfection. In the Otahuna Lodge, flawlessness flourishes. When you lead guests to their graceful suites, impress them with your astute choices from the seven lodges tucked comfortably within quaintly fashionable nineteenth-century architecture. Ornate, wood-burning fireplaces and stained-glass windows unobtrusively compete with newly carved woodwork and fine furnishings.

Suites are endowed with generous super-king beds, luxurious linens, and splendid bathroom amenities. Artwork commissioned especially for Otahuna Lodge gracefully competes for attention with flowers plucked fresh from the estate gardens. During recent restorations, entire bedrooms were redesigned as glorious baths that elevate the spirit of indulgence. Enjoy the summit your senses reach.

Food and wine take center stage when the clock chimes the hour to toast to your birth year. The inspired menu celebrates the best of fresh New Zealand produce with an emphasis on seasonal and estate-grown offerings. Uncluttered flavors and singularly tasteful ingredients are the hallmarks of an Otahuna table. Private tables in the sunken wine cellar, the intimate library, and the drawing room turret all vie for the honor of hosting your affair. Linger for days, and experience them all.

Top off your party with a dance in the lovely ballroom. Cathedral ceilings suspend high over the setting. Intimate enough for closeness, but sufficiently large for sixty-four, the doors open to imaginative dining and dancing. Friends may wonder what you plan for the rest of your life. Keep them guessing.

One of Rhodes's greatest legacies—the thirty acres of Otahuna manicured lawns and rambling, semi-wild woodlands—gives vent to wandering spirits. Seasonal daffodils accompany outside adventures. Stroll the restored pathways of century-old woodlands or strike up a tennis match on the spacious courts. When wider horizons beckon, horseback riding and bicycling answer the call. The architectural gems and botanical gardens of Christchurch are only minutes away. The world-class Tai Tapu golf courses entice competition with the pros. For the courageous, driving the dramatic crater rim of an extinct volcano thrills the daredevils, so make certain they know the hour to return.

Begin a new year in your life within the intimate warmth of a Colonial mansion where state-of-the-art design meets old-world craftsmanship. Discover the delight of tradition with a twist.

"The coastline awakens each morning
to glorious adventure and closes each night
in candlelit elegance."

Family Recipes

Places Family and Friends Adore

The Inn
at Perry Cabin

The lure of a luxury inn with an enthralling history and a galaxy of goings-on brings your family together to create a new legend. Just beyond the small town of St. Michaels, Maryland, the elegant nineteenth-century mansion resides on twenty-five lush acres overlooking the magical water-world on the eastern shore of Chesapeake Bay. Your family can arrive easily from any direction and can even fly in to the helipad. All roads lead to the Inn at Perry Cabin.

The coastline awakens each morning to glorious outdoor adventures and closes each night in candlelit elegance. An overabundance of open-air exploits abounds, including sail-boating, fishing, and biking. Host a picnic and play croquet. Not far away, quaint antique shops and boutiques line Main Street. On the bay, charter a fishing boat, pick up a water taxi, or board a sunset cruise at the Inn's marina. Finding time to experience all of it may be the challenge.

Take your group portrait in front of the state's oldest holly tree beside the front entrance. The two-hundred-year-old tree serves as the official Christmas tree of St. Michaels, a perfect backdrop to record for posterity every generation in your family tree. Once your guests cross the velvety lawn, they may vie for the perfect room inside. Lavish contemporary and antique

furnishings surround a cozy, crackling fireplace where listening to a retelling of the inn's history may be difficult due to the distracting opulence. A softly lit, decidedly romantic evening atmosphere compliments a casual and nautical daytime motif. Think Ralph Lauren meets Norman Rockwell.

English and American antiques decorate the guestrooms and suites. Plush Italian marble tile and Frette linens provide homey touches. Second floor rooms offer French doors that lead onto decks, patios, or verandas for relaxing and remembering days gone by. Fireplaces and separate living areas invite quiet moments for reflection. No one will mind being completely spoiled.

Laugh about old times and describe new adventures during the traditional family meal when everyone comes together. Up to twenty guests can fill the long, polished wooden table in the private dining room. The chefs in Sherwood's Landing ensure that each person experiences unparalleled dining. Suit everyone's tastes with the ritual of richly prepared special meals and unforgettable deserts.

Whether you and your guests explore the town and historic neighborhoods or nestle in an Adirondack chair on the lawn and watch the boats pass by, the ties that bind pleasantly unite you at the Inn at Perry Cabin.

The Ritz-Carlton, Grand Cayman

*T*reasure the time you spend together at your next family reunion. The irresistible lures of sun, sand, and cosmopolitan attractions enthusiastically draw one and all to the sparkling waters of the Caribbean Sea. The Ritz-Carlton shines like a star over Grand Cayman, the largest island in a trio of tropical treasures. Call your family members to gather at the plush hotel on Seven Mile Beach, where barefooting holds forth as a way of life.

Guests feel a sense of suspended time the moment they cross the gleaming stretch of sand washed by gentle ocean waters and behold the 144-acre resort that stretches from the sea to the North Sound. Temptations to play, rejuvenate, nourish, and celebrate are as numerous as starfish on the beach. Take the group portrait early, or everyone may forget.

Once inside, new standards of luxury hold court. The soothing sanctuary offers distinctive amenities, a dedicated staff, and design touches that overwhelm the senses. Your group can choose from an engaging array of rooms. Incomparable considerations adorn each exquisite setting. Some of you may seek the grandest level of relaxation and extravagance by calling one of the residential villas your home away from home. Several bedrooms, a chef's kitchen, and a spacious

terrace dare you to forget the beach, Greg Norman golf course, and restaurants just beyond your door. When you are inside the Ritz-Carlton, the call of nature competes with the lure of luxury.

Talk about your adventures during a superb dinner. Top chefs delight every palate with their culinary ingenuity, passion, and talent for celebrating the many ways to serve fish and steaks. An opulent Sunday brunch raises indulgence to a new level in the signature restaurant Blue by Eric Ripert. Periwinkle offers inventive seafood in an alfresco ambiance,

and guests can dine all day overlooking the sea, as 7 produces evening steaks that compete for attention with the dramatic hues of the Caribbean sunset. Create matchless moments you can all reminisce about for years to come.

A welcome retreat for families, the Ambassadors of the Environment by Jean-Michel Cousteau introduces kids age four to seven to adventures in nature. Explore cities beneath the sea and secrets in the sand. The natural wonders of the Cayman Islands showcase exploration and active study within a natural classroom and living laboratory of fun eco-adventures.

Invite your guests to share your passion for water, wind, and racquets. Explore the island's famous underwater world, and then head out to the Courts to improve your backhand. The Ritz-Carlton's tennis facilities combine the legendary Ritz-Carlton name with coaching from legendary Nick Bollettieri pros.

Guests of all ages indulge in the area's wealth of water sports, shopping, and sightseeing, but the tranquility of Silver Rain, a La Prairie Spa, entices some of you to remain behind, while the rest of your gang takes to the outdoors. The pampering of a healing massage restores your well-being.

The idyllic tropical paradise of the Ritz-Carlton, Grand Cayman, brims with historic island charm, modern conveniences, and nightlife. Tell everyone to meet you on the island where highflyers come to lie low, billionaires go barefoot, and iguanas have the right of way.

Winterlake Lodge

The family that loves the outdoors and craves a getaway from city life needs no persuasion to gather at Winterlake Lodge and head for the trails. Embark on a journey to another world where awesome accommodations, seclusion, spectacular scenery, and adventures abound.

Sequestered along Alaska's historic Iditarod Trail, the lodge lies 198 trail miles northwest of Anchorage atop a small bluff overlooking the lake. A vaulted cathedral ceiling with soaring, two-story windows frames the main lodge against the snowcapped peaks beyond. Your guests can land by floatplane in the summer or ski-plane in the winter. Tell them to come prepared for world-class sport fishing, canoeing, kayaking, rafting, and mountain biking.

Outdoorsmen are at home in the trapper cabins spread out on fifteen acres overlooking Winterlake and the northern lights. The log construction harks back to old Alaskan bush homes, and the handmade furniture invites your family to relax and reminisce. If you snooze while the temperature tops out in the early afternoon, the woodstoves never go out. Guides gladly stoke them for you.

Have you ever seen a Chocolate Lily? The uncommon perennial blooms in the spring when Winterlake Lodge transforms into a luxury chalet bursting with rare flowers, berries, and birds. Just behind the villa, Wolverine Mountain paints the perfect canvas for your group to assemble for their reunion photo.

The humdrum world seems strangely dim after wellness instructors guide you through daily yoga, meditation, and stretching classes. A hot tub on the deck and a lakeside, wood-burning sauna heat up perfect pastimes to close a day spent floating on Happy River and fishing in Canyon Creek. You may need an invigorating massage in the wellness room after extended hiking around Red Lake. Surrender yourself to absolute pleasure.

Get the reunion off to a roaring start with a family dinner of traditional Alaskan regional fare or in the spacious bar where wine, appetizers, and a game area dare the demure. And before you turn in for the evening, sit on the porch and watch the eagles fly over the stunning views of the Trimble and Hayes glacier and the beginnings of the Rainy Pass. At Winterlake Lodge, your doorstep opens to the reunion of a lifetime.

Burrawang West Station

A successful family reunion calls for a unique location, delicious dining, action-packed activities, and a chance to relax and get acquainted with those you love. Legendary Burrawang West Station packs all this into a unique blend of traditional elegance and country hospitality. Call everyone to rally to the majestic beauty. The timeless landscape feels like home as it should be.

Australia's most accessible and authentic outback experience stretches across twelve thousand acres of Lachlan River country in Central New South Wales. You arrive after a short flight or leisurely drive from Sydney across the scenic Blue Mountains. The magnificent country estate surrounds you in peaceful, picturesque luxury. Grant your family the opportunity to discover each other and create enduring memories.

Those traveling a long distance will be relieved to find that the Station offers a charming and serene respite. Break the ice with an informal gathering beside the fireplace in the living room, billiard rooms, bar, or cellar. Enjoy the inviting warmth of the farm, the overwhelming vastness of the landscape, and its ever-changing moods. An Aussie yarn-spinning champion draws everyone near to be regaled with an amazing, rip-

roaring tale. Unwind and lose yourself in close-knit family laughter.

Get people talking, sharing, and having fun with your first dinner together. Feeding a large group of people with different tastes comes easily at Burrawang West Station. Award-winning chefs create outstanding cuisine to make big family meals a treat. The expert chefs surprise you with some of the finest, lip-smacking platters prepared from Burrawang's fresh herb and vegetable gardens. From fine dining in formal surroundings to casual, alfresco eating, they specialize in fulfilling your pleasures.

Fire up a roaring barbecue poolside and let everyone enjoy the robust fare. A full, open bar keeps spirits high. At a Burrawang West Station family reunion, you get your yearly slice of everyone's history, a good dose of tall tales, and a gander at the year's crop of new babies.

Gather your energy for the fantastic experiences about to happen. Burrawang West Station provides twelve spacious suites spread over four intriguing lodges. The suites are beautifully decorated with impressive artwork and traditional Australian antique furnishings. Each suite has an adjoining

sitting room with flaming fireplace, a cozy kitchenette, and a fully screened veranda for enjoying the sweeping billabong views.

A comfy night leads to an exhilarating morning. Prepare for fun times from whip-cracking lessons with masterful stockmen to quad bike adventures. Enjoy watching your family take to the countryside and escape to the floating pontoon where adventuresome ones can find a canoe and set adrift on the Yarrabandai billabong. Swing clubs on the par-three, putt-and-chip golf holes complete with tee, fairway, and bunkers. A day at Burrawang mustering sheep and spotting kangaroos satisfies every whim with abundance.

When the day glides gracefully to an end, stargaze through the telescope in the observation tower. Observe your daring ones taking a hot air balloon ride silhouetted against the sinking sun. Magic fills the air at a champagne sunset where truly over-the-top experiences have made for memorable events everyone will recall for decades.

Jeweled horizons hang a perfect backdrop to record a portrait that highlights the grand spirit of your relations. Immortalize your connection at Burrawang West Station.

Sun Boat IV

$\mathcal{I}$f Cleopatra and the rest of her relatives reassembled today, the largest of Abercrombie & Kent's fleet of Nile cruise ships would fittingly ferry the family home to the banks of the Nile Valley. The Sun Boat IV has been completely modernized, transforming its formerly graceful, quiet tones into vibrant, bold splashes of Art Deco. The geometric forms and decorative elements found in ancient Egyptian art decorate every room. Marc Antony would revel in the new designs, and when your family gathers, the assembly can lay claim to all the treasures of Egypt. If your clan craves a quest for adventure, the journey begins here.

Teak flooring splendidly spreads across five spacious decks, and the Egyptian marble flooring on the sun deck reflects a scene fit for a queen. Sun Boat IV contains two Presidential Suites, two Royal Suites, and thirty-six luxury cabins for unsurpassed comfort. Plunge pools, perfect for a refreshing dip under brilliant Egyptian skies, entertain the hearty. The ship's inviting lounges give everyone a setting in which to relax, talk of old times, and plan for the future.

Sit on the boat's fantail and watch desert life drift by, as Nubian music floats harmoniously from the river shore.

Attentive staff caters to your beck and call, while you prepare to moor on private docks at Luxor, Aswan, and Kom Ombo. If you were born to sail the Nile, this spacious ship may be so alluring that you hesitate to disembark. The new Sun Boat IV unveils countless pleasures to keep even the most adventure-minded members of your group entertained.

Surrender to the temptation to tour treasure-filled tombs in the Valley of the Kings. A signature itinerary tailor-made for your group offers an excursion as only Abercrombie & Kent can create. Their deep roots in Egypt and long-established relationships provide a degree of access and insight no other operator can match.

Return from the ancient temples to the comforts of Sun Boat IV. Spacious and well-decorated outward-facing cabins all afford excellent views of the Nile River banks. Look out on robed figures romantically riding camels profiled against the twilight sky. Marvel at the land where ancient legends and mystery flourish as they did in the time of the Pharaohs. In some places, the site stirs you. On the Sun Boat IV, the cruise caresses you.

Sundance Resort

*A*s family trees develop, reunions grow as gigantic as a Hollywood epic. When your reunion calls for an intimate, easygoing hideaway, the Sundance Village of film-festival fame stages a setting where your family become close in ways you never imagined.

Invite your family to the Sundance Resort along the north fork of Provo Canyon in Utah. At the base of Mount Timpanogos, the majesty of more than six thousand acres spreads out rustic chic committed to the balance of art, nature, and recreation. Pamper your loved ones, take part in your favorite activities, and try daring new feats. Discover delights together in a world of stirring mountains and inspiring valleys.

Your family finds ways to come together because your roots go as deep as Utah trees. Founded by Robert Redford in 1969, Sundance Resort achieves understated sophistication in the rarified air of spectacular mountains. Summers spring to colorful life with widespread wildflowers, and heavenly snow blankets whimsical winters. When your family flocks to Sundance, opportunities for adventure, exploration, and intimacy charm away any memory of city life.

Sundance may spotlight celebrities during its annual film festival, but in winter, the ski slopes earn all the applause.

Swoosh down spectacular ski runs, and in the warm havens of slopeside lodges, reshape the generational values your family holds dear.

Relatives stay connected within welcoming mountain cottages that echo the simplicity of the natural setting. Rough-hewn beams, stone fireplaces, and woodstoves luxuriously offer total comfort. At the end of an adventurous day, remember old times in front of a glowing fireplace, or snuggle into beds and sleeping lofts topped with colorful duvets. The Native American-style cottages boast soaring cathedral ceilings and gorgeous views of the snowy fir and aspen groves nestled in the serenity of mountain woods.

At Sundance, loved ones never feel as if they are traveling. Spend entire days enjoying a kaleidoscope of activities. Thrill to ski and snowboard on dozens of immaculately groomed runs. Sundance's team of instructors even teaches children and grandparents how to navigate the gentler slopes. Take a hot chocolate break at the Bearclaw lodge with 360-degree views of the mountains. For slower-paced fun, simply ride the chairlifts up into the breathtaking peaks. Truly relax, while the snow enthusiasts have a blast.

Few places in the world have the majesty, beauty, and convenience of Sundance in the summer. The full roster of warm-weather activities includes full-moon lift rides, mountain biking, hiking, and horseback riding. Sundance has over ten miles of alpine hiking trails meandering over steep terrain.

Nine local golf courses, daredevil skiing, and fly-fishing create booming appetites. Rally one and all to recount their adventures at a dinner in the Tree Room. Bountiful buffets and midnight menus give your group the opportunity to enjoy all their favorites. Each meal becomes a savory, multi-course affair.

Entice your loved ones to a memorable reunion in the storybook villages of Sundance, where family and togetherness go hand in hand with nature.

"Prepare for a scintillating retreat."

No Pictures Please

The Splurge before Your Wedding

Hotel Fasano

Brazilians know how to bring flair to a singles' party. The hallmark of trendsetting hospitality shines in the heart of Ipanema Beach, where the Hotel Fasano transforms Rio de Janeiro's most coveted address with modernity and efficiency in design and service.

Upon arrival, your companions experience the stunning sensation of a greeting beneath a capricious pekia tree towering over the lavish lobby. Retro designs from the 1950s and 1960s gloriously reverberate within a maze of architectural wonders, warm earthy tones, and a wealth of surprises. These whimsical details herald the launch of a party no one will ever forget.

Be the bright stars amid the place to see and be seen. Your festivity in the most fashionable hotel in one of the world's most stimulating cities shows that you have your friends' best interests at heart. The added allures of exciting Ipanema beaches invite everyone to fun-filled days sharing laughter.

Hotel Fasano combines chic sophistication with warm rooms for the partygoers. Breathtaking suites boast private balconies with sweeping views of the Ipanema beach and Two Brothers Mountain. Inside, sensual details such as

king-size beds draped in dreamy Egyptian cotton linens and goose-down pillows invite one and all to slip into sumptuous surroundings. Although the Rio waters beckon, beach watching from the rooftop infinity pool keeps the fast-paced party together. Surround your friends with the best in new-age eye candy.

Let them eat cake and appetizers and dinners. Rogério Fasano sets a new standard for traditional Italian-style dining in a casual atmosphere overflowing with explosive good times. The menu explores the most diverse aspects of Mediterranean seafood cuisine, and breakfasts, lunches, and dinners are seasoned with stimulating imagination.

Hot dishes and well-wishes are the right way to celebrate the final days before a wedding.

Take your entourage out for glorified good times. Rio de Janeiro boasts hip and cool clubs and restaurants. Nonstop shopping for the girls extends to nearly every corner of the city. For the bachelors, plan high-adrenaline adventures with white-water rafting, skydiving, and rock climbing escapades. Give thrill-seekers a chance to dare the devil. At Fasano, a last hurrah has no limits.

The fabulous Hotel Fasano never fails to be modern and chic. Bring the excitement of Rio into a backdrop for your bash, and turn the town upside down.

The Beverly Hills Hotel

*L*egends are created here. Before your wedding, fashion your own fable with festivities in the privacy and tranquility of what some call the "Pink Palace." The Beverly Hills Hotel may be a place to see and be seen, or to catch glimpses of famous faces, but the splendor of twelve acres of lush, tropical gardens, exotic flowers, and private walkways attracts more than celebrities. Entice your entourage to a hotel where everyone raves about the comfort, spaciousness, and beauty.

A superlative combination of service, location, and architecture makes the Beverly Hills Hotel stand out like a star in a crowd of extras. More dramatically beautiful than ever, the expansive grace of the magnificent property has all the right elements to raise your celebration to the height of a happening. The California lifestyle rules that blue jeans and diamonds are an impressive combination in a setting where exclusivity and privacy are as important as a red-carpet welcome. Strike a pose. People will notice.

The famous pool and cabanas host more stars than there are in Hollywood. The California landscaping beckons attention, but all eyes will be on you from the moment you come into view. At the Beverly Hills Hotel, you can revel in

a party palace, be whatever you want to be, and fulfill your every expectation. If only real life was as obliging.

Your time in the spotlight extends to an evening of eminence within the hotel's guest rooms, suites, and legendary bungalows. Rooms are designed to feel spacious, timeless, and comfortably elegant. A colorful palette of distinctive Beverly Hills accents radiates brighter than stars at the Academy Awards. All furnishings have been custom-designed including canopied beds. Comforters made with matelassé fabric, velvet throw pillows, and magnificent artwork make every room inimitable. Different patterns of fabrics, draperies, and textures complete the mosaic of hues. When bold innovation meets exquisite design, your guests feel like superstars.

The specialty suites and bungalows attract approval with private entrances, living areas with baby grand pianos, fireplaces, and huge lounge terraces. Immaculate restorations have transformed the historic Paul Williams Suite to its former elegance, and the Presidential Suite has a private entrance opening to 2,500 square feet of living space. Bungalow 5 boasts four bedrooms and a private lap pool. An adjoining kitchen, a personal twenty-four-hour chef and butler, and a Jacuzzi bath with separate his and hers showers bring peerless perfection to you. Size does matter.

The film capital recognizes its best with an Oscar. Bestow an award on the Beverly Hills Hotel for fulfilling their promise of glamour and grandeur for your special occasion.

Victoria House

Paradise was never lost. Take pleasure in a prelude to the wedding you worked so hard to achieve. Invite your friends to a land of unspoiled beaches and tall swaying palm trees. An endless azure sea embraces two of the world's hidden gems: the magnificent Belize barrier reef and the Victoria House. Two charming private villas set among tropical gardens of bougainvillea, hibiscus, and oleander entice you to be as laid back as you desire and as adventurous as you dare.

Enter Victoria House and kick off your shoes. The island playground reminds you of a plantation surrounded by nineteen lush unspoiled acres of gardens. The Caribbean unfolds its timeless rhythms just a stone's throw away, and the two villas boast beautiful sea views. Irresistible diving, dining, swimming, and snorkeling keep you constantly in your bathing suit. Anticipate barefoot chic under the San Pedro sun.

Guests find paradise in a villa just a few steps from the water's edge where the tide ebbs and flows in cadence with your moods. The Casa Del Sol entices single men into a spacious five-bedroom home offering a master bedroom with a bamboo queen-size bed and a large bathroom with a Mexican-style walk-in shower. The living room, dining room, and kitchen all

open to an oversized, covered veranda furnished with wicker and mahogany furniture. Upstairs, two privately accessed bedrooms each with an en-suite bath, air-conditioning, and king-size beds share a balcony that overlooks the beach.

The spacious and bright two-bedroom Casa Playa Blanca villa, with vaulted hardwood ceilings, blends comfortable indoor space with the white sand of the palm-shaded beach. When sunrise breaks over the barrier reef, dazzling rays also illuminate the Casa Del Sol next door. The spacious plantation-style home encompasses playful living spaces and enticing Caribbean views.

Comfortable but casual dining remains a popular favorite at Victoria House. Sumptuous breakfasts overlooking the pool begin each day with appetizing surprises, and dinners accompanied by the ocean's caressing waves give your guests endless varieties of cooked-to-order seafood. Match meals with fine wines imported from France, Australia, and Napa. The Admiral Nelson Bar always invites those in your group to celebrate on the wraparound veranda anytime of the day or night.

When wedding bells ring, treat the bachelors and bachelorettes to one last bash. Get out, get wet, and get wild with the year's hottest party inside Victoria House.

101 Hotel

For couples wanting to express gratitude to members of their wedding in a playful and adventurous destination, exciting possibilities resound throughout the 101 Hotel in Reykjavík, Iceland. It wears a crown named after the fashionable nightlife district in the heart of downtown.

Conjure music, drinking, dance, and fun. Iceland can be best described as young, daring, and mystical. Spouting geysers, tumbling waterfalls, towering mountains, and magical lakes enchant you with a rare feeling of utter tranquility. Reykjavík may seem like a tiny seaside village set as a jewel in a necklace of unspoiled nature, but plenty of cultural happenings bolster its reputation as a hotbed of legendary nightlife under northern lights.

In appreciation and gratitude for your friends' participation in your wedding, treat them to an exciting affair where everyone feels comfortable. The five-story, thirty-eight-room 101 Hotel sparkles as an oasis of contemporary style.

Bestow a whimsical touch on your merrymaking. Rather than being fooled by its eastern bloc exterior, anticipate your astonishment when you see the interior painted with volcanic black, white, and ash gray. Expect an art gallery with every

design and detail carefully worked out to relax you. Corridors are dimly lit to create a sense of serenity. You wish to be a sensation. Achieve the impression fully within the 101.

Extra extravagances add up to one tremendous event. Intriguing Icelandic artworks from the owner's personal collection embellish the heart of the hotel. The most dramatic, a wall composed entirely of gently bulging shapes, soars to several stories and can be viewed from the glass-roofed bar and several of the guest rooms.

Though thoroughly modern, the 101 spared no expense in the commitment to the time-honored tradition of homey coziness. Bedrooms within the thirty-eight rooms and suites are light, airy, and open. Your friends will talk endlessly about the startling combination of maximum comfort and minimalist design. Enjoy hearing them chat enthusiastically about your tastes and the 101's personalized attention.

Dining in the 101 Bar and Restaurant draws everyone into an atmosphere where hamburgers and world-class cuisine sit side by side on the menu. An effortless combination of contemporary Icelandic and international cuisines engages your group to savor dishes served up by the restaurant that is all the rage in town.

Carry the party festivities out to an exclusive tour of intriguing Iceland in a "Golden Circle" route to view Langjökull, the awesome glacier; Mt. Hekla, a prominent and active volcano; and the Hjálparfoss, a wondrous waterfall. When the sun dips beyond the horizon and the moon heralds the rise of evening delights, unpack your dancing shoes and dress for revelry in a multitude of clubs and cafés. Iceland can be hot with a wide array of after-the-party pleasures.

The 101 Hotel creates a flawless setting for a wedding party. Get the party started.

Mandarin Oriental Hotel, New York

*L*ove changes the world. Everyone realizes you know what you want out of life when you invite people to a celebration at the Mandarin Oriental Hotel in New York. The glass towers lay claim to the best bite of the Big Apple. You anticipate your wedding get-together to be one of your life's most momentous events. Your friends want you to have the best life can bring. In the beating heart of the city, their company makes every day a celebration.

The Manhattan skyline at sunrise takes your breath away. No place on earth can compete with the impressive northwest arc of Columbus Circle overlooking Central Park. The Mandarin Oriental welcomes you into a discreet marble anteroom off West 60th Street. Supersonic elevators gracefully whisk you skyward, and then doors open to a glamorous lobby flanked by handblown glass sculptures that remind you of a magnificent crystal bouquet. You expect every detail of your party, no matter how minute, to be perfectly accomplished. Your dreams have led you in the right direction.

Choosing the Mandarin Oriental shows you have incredible taste, but the fabulous location alone does not fully illustrate your well-wishes. Plush rooms overlooking either the park or the Hudson River convince your friends that they are

in a special place at this extraordinary time. Asian influences flavor the suites with rich silks, luxurious wool and cotton fabrics, exotic woods, and fresh flowers.

Give everyone great reasons to smile when you invite them to share your stay in the Oriental Suite. A symphony of blue, gray, and gold, the large master bedroom, bath, and living and dining areas compete for attention with the separate study that doubles as an entertainment room. State-of-the-art technology delivers the ultimate film experience for an evening spent screening the latest blockbuster. Party on, while the mixture of New York and Oriental influences wraps you in a theater of your own.

Toast to a happy lifetime for the two of you in the Lobby Lounge, where you bring New York into your lap. Cocktails blend dramatically with the stunning panorama of Central Park and the Manhattan skyline when seen through a wall of windows that greet your partygoers as soon as they flow into the modern blend of Art-Deco chic and the luxuriously cozy ambiance. Manhattan looks marvelous from thirty-five stories high.

View the fairytale skyline from popcorn-yellow leather lounge seats in Asiate, the Mandarin Oriental's contemporary restaurant. Relish the chef's innovative Japanese-French cuisine, and then embrace companions in a lively atmosphere for after-dinner drinks. Savor sips of the bar's signature MOpolitans and MOtinis. Shared joys may well be the whole point of your party.

The Mandarin Oriental's spa provides every occasion for pampering. An oasis of amethyst crystal steam rooms, Asian-inspired treatment suites, and a panoramic, naturally-lit indoor lap pool give focus to rebalance. Enhance everyone's sense of well-being, and prepare for playing all your favorite games.

Devote time to your friends. Explore Central Park or shop world-class outfitters on Fifth Avenue. At night, cruise piano clubs and entertainment lounges and thrill to great stars on Broadway. At the Mandarin Oriental, the pulse of the action surrounds you.

Have a blast in the world's greatest city.

"Tell the one you love that the best years
of your lives are just ahead."

Let's Do It Again

Hideaways Offering New Memories

La Villa Gallici

Your anniversary has always been the best opportunity of the year to show your partner the intensity of your love. Take a romantic getaway to a town that has endured as the two of you have. Celebrate your marriage high above a magical city at Villa Gallici, a treasured seventeenth-century house in the heart of Aix en Provence in southern France. Paintings by Paul Cézanne often depicted the same soft, golden light that bathes the timeless beauty of the residence. Allow the radiance to inspire the two of you to remember why you first fell in love.

Take a moment to delight in your love's reflection in the pool by the Florentine garden before you venture inside. Reaffirm your commitment to each other as you enter a realm where the delicate fragrance of lavender floats in the matching golden light of the lounges. The hotel carefully displays Provençal period pieces, creating an incomparable, royal-court atmosphere. Your suite ensures a relaxing stay in rooms with every modern comfort, and the surroundings glow with the self-indulgent, sophisticated richness of Louis XV furniture and antique fabrics. Engage in unforeseen whims on a terrace and private

garden. Linger with an aperitif in the shade of cypress trees. Anticipate the unexpected.

Experience the charming world around Villa Gallici. A journey to the heart of Aix begins at the Cours Mirabeau, a beautiful, tree-lined avenue with over-hanging plane trees. Linger at one of the French sidewalk cafés, where warm air and sublime light magnify the feelings the two of you have for each other. The elegant boutiques in the Mazarin Quarter offer plenty of opportunities to pick up a sentimental keepsake the two of you will remember forever.

After you spend an afternoon holding hands, surprise your love with sun-kissed hours beside the pool before you set the mood for an intimate evening in the Villa Gallici's restaurant. The atmosphere of a cozy living room and traditional Provençal cuisine accompanied by the finest Bordeaux, Burgundy, and Aix wines makes for a great evening. Evoke wonderful memories lit by candles, as you did in the early days when you first dated.

The spectacular Villa Gallici holds you in a spellbinding oasis, a quiet and unpretentious retreat. When something stirs in your heart, just follow your instinct.

Bulgari Hotel-Bali

Anniversaries arrive one day and fleetingly leave the next. This time, savor the date with a longer journey. The Bulgari Hotel in Bali welcomes the two of you high upon a romantic plateau overlooking the Indian Ocean. You have told each other "I love you" many times. Say it again in a way that embraces the fullness of your union.

The wild Indian Ocean surf fills the air with the tang of the sea at this dramatically perched resort resting on a steep promontory high above a brilliant blue lagoon. The Bulgari's thatched-roof village escapes the ocean by a mere breath. Its fortress-like walls of white coral rock poise above one another on lushly landscaped terraces, giving the pleasant illusion that they all just happened. The splendor reminds you of why you fell in love.

Write a love note in the sand before you venture inside. The sentiment puts you in the mood for the breathtaking blend of Balinese and contemporary Italian accents about to overwhelm you. Architects have used indigenous stone and native wood finishes with irresistibly understated inspiration. Resplendent chambers make you yearn for more years filled with joy. The million-dollar views enfold each of the villas with fiery sunsets. Volcanic stone and sleek Bangkiray woods compose spacious bedrooms hugged by a study, dressing room, and black terrazzo bathroom enclosed in glass. Nothing matters but the two of you.

Show you remember and care with a romantic dinner in Il Ristorante. Toast to the triumph of your love, and savor the way chefs restyle Italian food and artfully display their dishes under the stars beside the cabana-fringed pool that appears to drift into the sea. In Il Ristorante, promises of adoration flow as freely as wine.

Give the gift of rejuvenation in the ancient Javanese spa, where lacy, carved teak walls surround a sanctuary of bridged reflection pools, an open-air relaxation lounge, and a yoga pavilion. The sea breeze billows through the curtains, and the soothing sounds of waves crashing on the beach sublimely relax you with the aromas of authenticity.

Good fortune brought the two of you together. Keep the fires burning with an unforgettable celebration at Bulgari, and your affection will bloom for all the days to come.

Hôtel Les Ottomans

*Y*our anniversary merits a glamorous and delightful time together. Turn the pages in the journal of your lives to a new chapter that begins at the Hôtel Les Ottomans. This tantalizing love nest cozies up to the banks of the mighty Bosphorus in Istanbul, a waterfront artistry of nature in a setting ranking in charm with the masterworks of men. One of the most gorgeous representations of Neo-Ottoman architecture, the residence was recently modernized as a lavish tribute to Istanbul's baroque revival, magnifying the inner poetry of the special reason for your journey.

Discover the remarkable dimensions of the Hôtel Les Ottomans' intricate ceilings, gold paintwork, and glistening chandeliers. Freely touch the Venetian velvet walls, precious antiques, and inspiring works of art. Respond to the peaceful vibrations of murmuring fountains that mark your passage into the realm of your private suite. If you desire an anniversary with storybook depth, the vaulted ceilings of the Saphir Suite and its promise of luxurious pleasure leave you breathless.

Awaken each morning to the splendid reality of the dreamy Bosphorus. The Ottomans' elegant wooden yacht harbors at their pier, ready to spirit the two of you on a thrilling journey into Istanbul bazaars and palaces. Your anniversary becomes an exhilarating occasion when you celebrate love and commitment in this timeless town.

Return to the Hôtel Les Ottomans' tantalizing Caudalie Vinotherapie Spa. Sink into the tranquility of the Turkish hammam, the liquid sound pool, the sauna, and the indoor swimming pool. Lose yourself in the ambiance of a rain forest, a soft thunderstorm, and a mountain setting. Melt into a Sauvignon massage or a Merlot scrub, and then relax in the meditation room. Nothing says "I love you" better than a personalized, tailor-made treatment for two.

Celebrate your life of love with international and Ottoman cuisines brilliantly merging with picturesque vistas of the Bosphorus banks in the exquisitely decorated Yali Hatun Restaurant. An imaginative range of ingredients gathered from the fertile vegetable and fauna gardens earmarks every evening for unexpected delights.

What makes you different from other couples has always been how well you complement each other. The Hôtel Les Ottomans invites you to step beyond to an especially meaningful rendezvous

Poetry Inn

The lifetime you have built together has lasted for years, as mature vineyards always produce delicious grapes season after season. On your anniversary, a gift alone can never prove your love. Harvest wonderful new memories by celebrating at the Poetry Inn. Whether the two of you enjoy simple pleasures indoors or lavish delights outdoors, the secluded and intimate Napa Valley retreat guarantees sweet togetherness for every taste.

A gated driveway opens off the Silverado Trail to receive you. A wood-burning fireplace welcomes you into the lobby decorated with dark woods and clean architectural lines. Live the life of a Napa Valley vintner and sip aged-to-perfection Cabernet on a private terrace, enjoying breathtaking panoramas of the wineries and palisades of the surrounding landscape as you make this anniversary the season of your life.

A mere five rooms envelope you with the simplicity of a small but charming environment. In the tranquil palatial space of the Grand Suite, a spectacular king-size bed draped with feather duvets and luxurious Italian linens resides beneath original artworks that celebrate the pastoral.

Delight your spouse with the sanctuary of a marble bathroom with a large soaking tub. Heated floors and a cozy wood-burning fireplace warm your thoughts. Enjoy the promise of more joyful years to come.

Gourmet, three-course breakfasts are served every morning. Begin the occasion with a breakfast of Brie-and-strawberry French toast at a table overlooking the valley. Dine in the commons area or savor the cuisine delivered to the comfort and privacy of your magnificent rooms. Whether your anniversary heralds your first or fiftieth year together, return your marriage to the honeymoon stage.

After a day touring the Napa Valley, visit the serene spa treatment rooms. Restore peace to your body and harmony to your mind. Share a relaxing aromatherapy spa day together and return ready to rejoice completely refreshed.

Sip a glass of fine wine from the inn's private cellar, and then drink in soothing views of the Napa countryside from your terrace. Turn down the lights, fire up some delicately scented candles, and create a dreamy, relaxing mood. At Poetry Inn, tell the one you love that the best years of your lives are just ahead.

Camp Jabulani

Baby elephants become easily bored, as do couples repeating the same old candlelight dinner on their anniversary date. This year, add some adventure to your commemoration with a jubilant journey to South Africa on a Camp Jabulani safari.

Tell your family, "It's all about the elephants." Inform them of your interest in the conservation and care of endangered wildlife while the two of you luxuriate in richly appointed suites, massive baths, and a private plunge pool. Keep secret the fact that you are surrounded by a La Prairie Spa and air-conditioning. Send home pictures of the two of you on canvas-covered saddles in a train of twelve elephants silhouetted against the sunset. Your family does not need to know that you have a butler to respond to your every request.

Welcome to the serenity of the African bush, where day and night, the cries in the wild are a symphonious background to elegant combinations of luxury and refinement. In the midst of untamed nature, enjoy a facial, a massage, and gourmet dining. By day, drive game with an experienced ranger, feed wild vultures, and trail elusive buffalos, lions, and leopards. When long shadows fall over the prairie, open a bottle of champagne on a rose-adorned table for two beneath the open stars. The chef personally introduces the menu at the start of each meal and stays to chat about the food. He creates perfectly sized portions of the freshest ingredients and presents them in an exquisite arrangement. With the panoramic view of the Drakensberg Mountains behind you, an anniversary in Africa will reinvigorate you.

Evenings in front of the fireplace with the love of your life define the essence of your spirit. A private lodge, sublime food, elegant décor, and charming staff see that the richness of organic elements creates a harmonious and pleasing balance between designed and authentic. An open flow of light and air allow for an untamed ambiance without forsaking optimum comfort. Curl up in comfort, secure in the knowledge that a minibar, ceiling fan, and electric blanket are as close as the calls of cheetahs.

Camp Jabulani perfectly translates the best of the African bush into a classic and graceful environment fit for princes and kings but warm as home. Commemorate your anniversary with the enchanting blend of elephants and elegance.

Relais Bernard Loiseau

*Y*our love has shined throughout the years. Let it glow vividly when you embark on the passionate passage of your anniversary celebration. Honor the hour at Relais Bernard Loiseau, an eighteenth-century post house residing midway between Paris and Lyon. A sensorial journey to commemorate your love and a renowned culinary experience unlike any other stirs up a blissful adventure for two.

Be thankful for another year to create memories together. Love takes on its full meaning in this timeless and magical atmosphere. The intimate character of this bourgeois mansion in the heart of the Morvan zealously stuns from every point of view. Ancient stones, antique terra-cotta tiles, and warm woods reflect the legacy of legendary Parisian palaces. The ambiance reminds you of your first flush of love.

Amble through the heart of the Chablis winemaking country or the famous vineyards around Beaune. Meander hand in hand along Auxois abbeys and medieval castles. Ride bikes through the wilds of the Morvan forests. Follow in the ancient footsteps of lovers gone by on the romantic trails surrounding magnificent Morvan Lake. Affection grows stronger every hour you spend together.

Make your world complete when you return to tender togetherness at Relais Bernard Loiseau. In a suite that overlooks the landscaped courtyard and garden, deepen your connection to the spirit you share. Antiques, polished stone floors, and beamed ceilings decorate the rooms with the same enduring elements that distinguish the strength of your devotion.

Gourmet diners flock to this idyllic country haven to savor the culinary delights, and first-timers are naturally distracted from the reason for their romantic interlude. The rustic dining room overlooks the landscaped garden, perfectly setting the stage for your celebration, but when the temptation to try Loiseau's best-known dishes takes hold of you, affection gives way to appetite.

Restore romance after dinner with any of the superb vintage wines from Relais Bernard Loiseau's seemingly endless wine cellars. Embrace your lover within the timeless allures of Relais Bernard Loiseau. The two of you achieved another milestone together. Rejoice in the love that brings you here.